Palgrave Studies in the History of Economic Thought

Palgrave Studies in the History of Economic Thought publishes contributions by leading scholars, illuminating key events, theories and individuals that have had a lasting impact on the development of modern-day economics. The topics covered include the development of economies, institutions and theories.

More information about this series at
http://www.palgrave.com/gp/series/14585

Mats Lundahl

The Dynamics of Poverty

Circular, Cumulative Causation, Value Judgments, Institutions and Social Engineering in the World of Gunnar Myrdal

palgrave
macmillan

Mats Lundahl
Stockholm School of Economics
Stockholm, Sweden

ISSN 2662-6578 ISSN 2662-6586 (electronic)
Palgrave Studies in the History of Economic Thought
ISBN 978-3-030-73346-9 ISBN 978-3-030-73347-6 (eBook)
https://doi.org/10.1007/978-3-030-73347-6

Cover illustration: Matteo Omied/Alamy Stock Photo

This Palgrave Macmillan imprint is published by the registered company Springer Nature Switzerland AG
The registered company address is: Gewerbestrasse 11, 6330 Cham, Switzerland

Preface

My first acquaintance with Gunnar Myrdal goes back to 1968, when he came to Lund, where at the time I was a business and economics student at the university. The occasion was the presentation of his three-volume *Asian Drama*, which was featured in the display window of the local bookstore. Myrdal spoke to a full house at the main venue of the student association and after his presentation he answered questions—in his own sweet way. 1968 was the year of the student revolt all over Western Europe. Myrdal was not known for being sympathetic to Marxists, so the representatives of the local brand did what they could to discredit his work as conventional and old-fashioned. Myrdal cut them short. He answered the first question with a counter-question: 'Who are you, and how old are you?' The interrogator replied with his age and added that he was a Bachelor of Arts. ''Bachelor of Arts?', retorted Myrdal. 'At your age I was already a professor!'

The second occasion that I saw Gunnar Myrdal was the only occasion that I met him face to face. It was also in Lund, on 7 June 1979, after having defended my Ph.D. thesis on the Haitian economy a week before. I had sent it to Myrdal in Stockholm and had received a letter, where he thanked me for 'the beautiful book', and said that he was going to a conference in Lund, organized by the geographer Torsten Hägerstrand. He had read my thesis and he wanted to see me. I was to call him at Hotel Lundia.

That left the question: 'At what time?' 'Myrdal is an old man', I told myself. 'He is certain to get up early.' So I called around eight. That was a fatal mistake. It was pandemonium. Alva was screaming in the background and I could not make sense of anything. We agreed that I should try later. In the meantime, I decided to go to the economics department before the next attempt. Once there, I found myself in the middle of chaos: 'Myrdal wants to see you! Myrdal wants to see you!' The great man was waiting for me for a late breakfast at the hotel.

When I got there and we had shaken hands, I complimented him for keeping on writing and publishing at his age. 'There is nothing else', he answered, bluntly. He asked me about my thesis, and I explained the somewhat intricate circumstances of how I had come to choose my exotic topic. 'Well, you have some shit in there [meaning algebra]' he said, 'but I would have given you a very high grade.' Imagine if I felt proud! 'Who was your supervisor?' 'Bo Södersten', I answered. 'Bah, Södersten; in my days it was world names: myself, Ohlin and Erik Lindahl.' After that he only talked about himself and his works. He asked me: 'Have you read my *Monetary Equilibrium*?' I replied that I had, since I had used the idea of circular, cumulative causation in my book.[1] 'Well', said Myrdal, 'that's a book about Wicksell, a book that Wicksell himself could have written, if he had only thought as clearly as I.'

The present book has its origin in a book chapter I had to write on Myrdal for an anthology on poverty. The chapter format was 20–25 pages, but I quickly realized that there was no way to accomplish that in a single go. Myrdal's wrestle with methodology extended across his entire academic life, from his doctoral dissertation to the very end, not only through the works dealing with poverty, but through virtually everything he wrote. In other words: I had to read all his major books, articles and book chapters, distilling them little by little into an essay. The thought dawned on me to write a longer work as well: a work that allowed for a more detailed examination of Myrdal's evolution as a methodologist and of his applications to important empirical questions in a series of magnificently conceived books.

[1] Lundahl (1979, Chapter 3).

Or as he put it himself, 'Our journals yield a crop of ever more minute studies, lacking in attempts toward that integration into a view of the whole social system which is the sine qua non of the institutionalists.'[2]

I am grateful to Peter Gavelin, Ute Harris and Clara Lindström at the library of the Stockholm School of Economics for their never-ending support. Thanks are also due to three anonymous referees for constructive comments to a first draft of the book. I hope I have lived up to their expectations in my revision. If not, it is entirely my own fault.

Djursholm, Sweden Mats Lundahl
December 2020

[2] Myrdal (1978a, p. 776).

Praise for *The Dynamics of Poverty*

"This will be the definitive study of the work of the great Swedish social scientist for a long time to come. It is based on detailed knowledge of the milieu that shaped Myrdal's life and thought as well as commanding scholarship over the extensive range of issues involved. We are all in debt to Mats Lundahl for this truly magnificent book."

—Ronald Findlay, *Ragnar Nurkse Professor Emeritus of Economics, Columbia University*

"This book provides the most comprehensive and readable survey of Gunnar Myrdal's economic reasoning, tracing it from his early education to old age. As a bonus the book also portrays reactions from critics on both sides of the political spectrum. This highlights how Myrdal intelligently interpreted a changing world without letting himself be fettered by ideological shackles."

—Stefan Fölster, *Director of Better Future Economics, grandson of Gunnar Myrdal*

"This is a fascinating and scholarly account of Gunnar Myrdal's lifelong struggle to understand fundamental social, economic and political forces. Lundahl traces how Myrdal, one of the most prominent social scientists of the 20th century, analyzed the population problem in Sweden in the 1930s, the racial issue in the United States in *An American Dilemma* in the 1940s and the development problem in the Third World in *Asian*

Drama in the 1960s. The book provides a concise synthesis of Myrdal's methodology as it developed over time – clearly a contribution of great interest to present-day debate on the tasks and challenges facing social scientists."

—Lars Jonung, *Professor Emeritus at the Knut Wicksell Centre for Financial Studies, Department of Economics, Lund University*

Contents

CHAPTER 1

Introduction: The Man and His Work

A Capsule Biography[1]

Gunnar Myrdal was born on December 6, 1898, in Skattungsbyn in the province of Dalarna, as Karl Gunnar Pettersson, but in 1914, his father changed the family name to Myrdahl, and three years later, Gunnar dropped the h. His father was a building contractor, which meant that the family frequently moved during Gunnar's childhood, until it ended up in Stockholm in 1914. Gunnar finished high school there in 1918, at the well-known Norra Real.

During his high school years, Myrdal made his first acquaintance with some of the works of the economists Gustav Cassel and Eli Heckscher, but also those of the political scientist Rudolf Kjellén, notably his stress of the subordinate role of the individual vis-à-vis society and his insistence that political science was essentially an instrumental discipline which could be

[1] No comprehensive biography of Gunnar Myrdal, dealing with both the man and his work, exists. The closest we get to that is Jackson (1990), which, in spite of the fact that it mainly deals with *An American Dilemma* (Myrdal 1944a), also offers insights about the periods before and after that. The short work of Barber (2008) deals mainly with the intellectual side. Cf. also the biographies of Gunnar and his wife, Alva, listed in note 2, Chapter 3, where the emphasis is more on the personal side. Here, I have mainly drawn on Gustafsson (1987–1989), Jackson (1990), Swedberg (1990), and Barber (2008).

M. Lundahl, *The Dynamics of Poverty*, Palgrave Studies in the History of Economic Thought,
https://doi.org/10.1007/978-3-030-73347-6_1

used to design interventions in society based on a political stance. Walter Jackson summarizes:

> During his gymnasium [high school] years, Gunnar Myrdal ... read the work of Swedish political thinker Rudolf Kjellén, a professor at Uppsala University and a member of Parliament for the Conservative party. Kjellén was a nationalist who deprecated class conflict, distrusted the masses, and preached a doctrine of the subordination of the individual to the state. In contrast to Swedish liberals, Kjellén argued that the citizens had a moral duty to place the collective welfare of the nation above the pursuit of their individual or group self-interest. Social science, for Kjellén, was inherently a political enterprise: the scientist did not seek an objective detachment from politics in order to discover scientific laws of human behavior; he actively participated in politics to guide the nation-state's development. Though Myrdal would quickly move beyond Kjellén's conservative positions, the Uppsala professor's collectivist, interventionist vision would remain in Myrdal's mind as an alternative to the laissez-faire doctrines that he would learn from his academic mentor, the liberal economist Gustav Cassel. Kjellén's geopolitical realism would be one of several influences on the young Myrdal's writing as he attempted to develop his own political viewpoint.[2]

His contact with Kjellén's works was Myrdal's first exposure to what he would later think of as social engineering. Another person that influenced him at the time—and for life—was his teacher John Lindquist, PhD in geography, who taught Swedish, geography and history, and who inculcated in his student the importance of the Enlightenment approach to society: that it was possible to reform both people and society, and pointed out to him that the social sciences were not objective but tainted by the personal views and preconceived notions of the observer, a position which, as we will find, would play a decisive role for Myrdal's approach to economics. In a tape recording from the 1980s, Myrdal expressed his admiration for Lindquist:

> My Swedish and history teacher, John Lindquist, would exert a special influence on me. He used to take time pacing in front of the class and speak about the Age of Enlightenment. It was there that I got this attitude towards the philosophy of Enlightenment, which I more and more came to

[2] Jackson (1990, p. 445).

> regard as a conviction, that the humans and their society could be reformed and become better.[3]

Lindquist appears to have been equally important when it came to the problem of objectivity in social research. The introduction of an essay that Myrdal wrote for him in 1917 about the Swedish king Gustav IV Adolf is revealing:

> The writing of history will never be so objective that the views and sympathies of the writer will not at least partly tinge it; they make his eye for certain eras and some parts of the times and the humans that he wants to portray that sharper or duller; they will affect the form, make the style more considerate or the other way round, with a single word create a partly false basic mood.[4]

When Gunnar Myrdal began his academic studies in the fall of 1918, his subject was not economics, but law. He received his Bachelor of Law degree in 1923, but—although he practiced it for a while, as a law clerk in the Stockholm municipal court, as a magistrate in the small town of Mariefred and as a public prosecutor in Norrköping—law was not his mission in life. In 1919, Gunnar met his future wife, Alva. née Reimer, whom he married in 1924. That was the beginning of an intellectual companionship that would last all the way until Alva's death in 1986. She put Cassel's *Theoretische Sozialökonomie*[5] into her fiancé's hands and encouraged him to take up economics instead.

So he did, precisely with Cassel at Stockholm College. Myrdal was admitted into Cassel's select group of predilected students, fell under his sway, obtained a grant to go to Germany and England, and finished his graduate years with his PhD thesis defense in 1927. Before that, however, he had begun to work on a project led by Gösta Bagge, financed by the Rockefeller Foundation, on wages, cost of living and national income in Sweden, which produced a book on the cost of living, published in 1933.[6] In 1929, Gunnar and Alva Myrdal went to the United States for

[3] Cited by Andersson (1989, pp. 22–23).

[4] Cited by ibid., p. 28.

[5] Cassel (1918).

[6] Myrdal (1933c).

the first, but not last, time of their lives, financed by Rockefeller Foundation scholarships, visiting a number of American universities and falling into a life-long love with the country.

Coming back to Sweden, Myrdal published two of his most important works, both of which we will come back to. The first one was *Vetenskap och politik i nationalekonomien* [*The Political Element in the Development of Economic Theory*],[7] where he demonstrated that he had absorbed what his high school mentor, Lindquist, had taught him. The second one was the Swedish edition of what in the end would become *Monetary Equilibrium*, a study of the approach of Knut Wicksell to monetary economics and policy, a decisive step in Myrdal's methodological development.[8]

The 1930s were a political decade for Gunnar Myrdal. He became a member of the Social Democratic Party in 1931, he was elected to Parliament in 1934 and he was increasingly involved in a number of governmental committees on economic and social issues: housing statistics, social aspects of housing, housing credit, population and agriculture. As we will come back to, he ran the population committee virtually on his own, in spite of not being its chairman.

Myrdal advanced fast academically. In 1933, he succeeded Gustav Cassel as Lars Hierta Professor of Economics and Finance at Stockholm College. The same year, he published *Konjunktur och offentlig hushållning* [Business Cycles and Public Economics] as part of the 1933 budget and finance bill of the Social Democratic government,[9] extended the following to *Finanspolitikens ekonomiska verkningar* [The Economic Effects of Fiscal Policy], for the Committee on Unemployment [Arbetslöshetskommissionen].[10] These two books were fundamental for the establishment in Sweden of an active, interventionist, fiscal policy, aimed at combating unemployment.

1934 was also the year when Gunnar Myrdal became known to all Swedes. The occasion was the publication of *Kris i befolkningsfrågan* [Crisis in the Population Question], which he wrote together with his wife, Alva.[11] The book, which was only nominally about the possible

[7] Myrdal (1930).

[8] Myrdal (1931a, 1939) respectively.

[9] Myrdal (1933a).

[10] Myrdal (1934).

[11] Myrdal and Myrdal (1934).

decrease of the Swedish population, presented a radical social reform program which involved a substantial redistribution program from the rich to the poor and in favor of families with many children and a series of social engineering measures intended to improve the lot of low-income earners. It became an instant—hotly debated—bestseller in Sweden. We will deal extensively with it.

Four years after the publication of the population book, the Myrdals left Sweden for the United States for the second time, this time for one of the most important endeavors in Gunnar's life: the investigation of what was at the time known as the American 'Negro problem', racial discrimination and poverty, what would become his most important work: *An American Dilemma*,[12] a work that not only made a mark in the history of the social sciences but also contributed to the cause of the civil rights movements in the United States for some twenty years.

When Gunnar Myrdal made it back home to his native Sweden, he once more became directly involved in politics, first, between 1943 and 1945, as a member of a commission that dealt with Sweden's commercial and cultural relations with transoceanic countries—the so-called America commission—thereafter, 1944–1945, as chairman of the commission in charge of planning the Swedish post-war economy—what became known as the Myrdal commission. Between 1945 and 1947, he served as Minister of Trade in the Social Democratic government that succeeded the government of national unity that Sweden had had during the war years.

In 1947, Gunnar Myrdal became the executive secretary of the newly established United Nations Economic Commission for Europe in Geneva, where he worked with the facilitation of East-West trade and supervised the production of surveys of the economic problems of Europe. He would remain there until 1957. During his ten years in Geneva, he also wrote prolifically on poverty and inequality in the international context, publishing *An International Economy*,[13] his 'Cairo lectures', *Development and Under-Development: A Note on the Mechanism of National and*

[12] Myrdal (1944a).

[13] Myrdal (1956a).

International Economic Inequality,[14] and his extension of them: *Economic Theory and Under-Developed Regions*.[15]

During the Geneva period, Gunnar Myrdal also prepared his next research project—the largest he ever undertook. The topic was poverty in South Asia and the project, financed by the Twentieth Century Fund, would in the end span more than a decade. The final result was the monumental *Asian Drama*.[16] In this book, Myrdal built on the methodology that he had developed for *An American Dilemma*, covering all conceivable aspects and mechanisms of poverty and inequality mainly in India and Pakistan but also in nine other countries in the region. The work became so extensive that Myrdal had to leave his policy conclusions for a separate work, published in 1970: *The Challenge of World Poverty*.[17]

Asian Drama turned out to be Gunnar Myrdal's last major research undertaking. During the rest of his active life, he kept coming back to the themes that he had developed from the 1930s to 1960s: poverty, inequality—domestically and internationally—the need for social engineering and planning and the role of—overt or covert—value judgments in the social sciences. In 1974, he was awarded the Sveriges Riksbank Prize in Economic Sciences in Memory of Alfred Nobel, a prize which he—much to his chagrin—shared with Friedrich Hayek: an outspoken advocate of the market economy.

Gunnar Myrdal's last years were characterized by an increasingly critical view of the contemporary society. His enthusiasm for planning began to wane and he turned against what he perceived as increasing bureaucratization and centralization of the welfare state that he had helped to construct. He also began to question the justification and design of the foreign aid to poor countries which he had warmly recommended a couple of decades before. His last few years were difficult, as he suffered from Parkinson's disease. Gunnar Myrdal died on May 17, 1987.

[14] Myrdal (1956b).

[15] Myrdal (1957a).

[16] Myrdal (1968).

[17] Myrdal (1970).

An Egocentric Workaholic

In his memoirs, Ernst Wigforss, Swedish Minister of Finance 1925–1926, 1932–1936 and 1936–1949, the leading ideologue and visionary of the Swedish Social Democracy during the twentieth century, offers a characteristic of Gunnar Myrdal. He portrays him as 'an unusual man', a talent which a lot of people reacted against. In our country, writes Wigforss, we

> ... do not have much of the suspicion, or even animosity, against academics and intellectuals that you cannot help noticing in a rather widespread American opinion. But it cannot be denied that the reactions against Myrdal sometimes have been such that you seem to find points in common with the situation in America. Mostly perhaps in an unreasoning antipathy against the versatile, hence unpredictable and in the end dangerous, kind of intelligence and the kind of intellectuals that Myrdal to an unusual degree personifies.
>
> It is not difficult to understand the distrust against him, who appears to think faster than others, and hence runs through different possibilities, perhaps considering having acquired a more comprehensive panorama, before you yourself have arrived at the first aspect.[18]

The egocentricity theme runs like a thread through the comments on Myrdal offered by people who knew him well, for example Paul Streeten:

> Gunnar Myrdal had a way of mainly quoting himself in his writings. This is not uncommon among academics ... but in his case it was not the result of vanity but of the fact that with inescapable logic he had to give his own ideas top marks, for if someone else's ideas were better, he would adopt them, If anything, the habit of self-citation reflected not vanity but egocentricity.[19]

'Gunnar's egocentricity was ... of an unusual kind', writes his daughter Sissela Bok: 'Of course, he thought that the world was circling around him. But his world was more spacious than most, so much richer in insights and possibilities, much more coherent. This made it much

[18] Wigforss (1980, p. 361).

[19] Streeten (1992, p. 118).

more fascinating to talk to him than to more doggedly small-minded egocentrics'.[20]

Sissela Bok's sister, Kaj Fölster, agrees:

> He was not cold, he had a strong personal charisma and plenty of charm. He was an encouraging interdisciplinary thinker, and made spaces open up when he spoke. He rapidly punctured intellectual dishonesty and had no respect for social privileges. He never spoke drily of economic problems; it was always about humans. His sharp powers of observation and knowledge of social history made his mistrust of the powers that be a support for the individuals and groups that he would feel deeply for.[21]

'He was not in any way a full-time egocentric. He behaved pretty normally towards others', states Torsten Gårdlund, one of Myrdal's students and collaborators.[22] As could be expected, however, Gunnar Myrdal's egocentricity grew over time. Walter Jackson summarizes his career in this respect until the late 1960s:

> Myrdal had always been an individualist with a unique and original perspective on most of the problems that he tackled. His formidable ego, brilliance, and toughness had enabled him to withstand enormous pressure from powerful interests and to propose bold reforms in Sweden, America, and within the United Nations. But Myrdal's early and mid-career had also been marked by a certain pragmatism and ability to gauge the spectrum of opinions within a particular country or institution or community of thinkers and to propose policies that were timely or that were just emerging on the horizon of possibility. He was now in his late fifties and sixties, no longer involved in the political life of Sweden or the UN, and not really part of a community of thinkers in any country. Lacking these anchors, Myrdal's egocentricity became all the more pronounced. The young outsider from Dalarna who had burst onto the Stockholm scene as an enfant terrible was still an outsider, an angry prophet warning the world of disaster if something were not done about the catastrophic problem of hunger and poverty in the Third World, and he missed no opportunity to lecture Americans and Western Europeans about the remedies that were needed. Myrdal became increasingly convinced of the correctness of his

[20] Bok (1987, p. 168).

[21] Fölster (1992, p. 54).

[22] Hederberg (2004, p. 82).

> views, and he frequently did not listen carefully to what other scholars in the field were saying. Even his admirers admitted that a conversation with Myrdal was difficult, that one had to be persistent and assertive to get one's ideas across to him. He had become, in Paul Streeten's words, an '*enfant terrible* emeritus'.[23]

Egocentricity far from always signals originality, but in Gunnar Myrdal's case it did. He turned his egocentricity into originality in research. And he lived for his research. Tore Browaldh, who was his assistant when he was in the United States for the 'America commission', studying the situation of the American economy and its future in his memoirs states: 'It is no exaggeration when Gunnar Myrdal says that work has given his life content and happiness. His production of lectures, articles and books has always been impressive …'[24] 'Nothing was done by halves', writes Charles Kindleberger in his obituary. 'His two most widely-known books, *An American Dilemma* (1944) and *Asian Drama* (1968), are blockbusters, 1500 and 2250 pages, respectively'.[25]

Paul Streeten shares the opinion of Browaldh and Kindleberger:

> Myrdal's work was his life. Although he sometimes talked as if he was not meant to write books but to dream under trees, drink wine and make love to girls, his work absorbed him totally, to the neglect of family, friends and hobbies. He was an avid reader of newspapers, but despised novels and light reading, and had little interest in recreations. His conversation was dominated by the subject on which he was working, and by discussion of political, economic and social developments in the world. Often he held forth in what amounted to a stream of consciousness, but then there would come an observation about the world, or a person, of amazing brilliance and originality. He combined warmheartedness and personal charm with an intolerance of anything that he saw as humbug or pomposity.[26]

[23] Jackson (1990, pp. 337–38). The quotation is from an unpublished manuscript by Streeten.

[24] Browaldh (1976, p. 55).

[25] Kindleberger (1987, p. 393).

[26] Streeten (1992, p. 120).

Scope of the Study

The present book—the contents of which are briefly outlined in the following—deals with Gunnar Myrdal's analysis of poverty, as applied to Sweden in the 1930s, the United States at the beginning of the 1940s, the international economy in the 1950s and South Asia in the 1960s. It also traces the development of the methodology which he applied in his main works, from the late 1920s to the beginning of the 1970s. As Paul Streeten has pointed out, 'Methodological questions occupied Myrdal's thought throughout his life'.[27] From the 1930s, so did poverty: its causes, consequences and remedies. The two themes are intimately interwoven in Myrdal's works. His methodology was completely central to what he wrote on poverty and social policy.

When fully developed, Myrdal's analysis rested on five interconnected pillars. The first is the principle of circular, cumulative causation, which in turn is based on the assumption that the analysis must be dynamic, and not static. The third is the conviction that the analysis must be carried out within an institutional framework. The remaining two pillars are explicit value premises and social engineering. The following constitutes an investigation of how, little by little, frequently in works that were dealing with completely different matters, Myrdal arrived at an approach which, along the way, he brought to bear on various social themes, until his research culminated in the monumentally conceived *Asian Drama*, published in 1968, and its sequel, *The Challenge of World Poverty*, from 1970.[28]

Myrdal was a heterodox economist all his life, more so during his later years than in his youth. It is evident already in his doctoral dissertation from 1927 that he was uncomfortable with the dominant neoclassical paradigm, which he felt was too static and too obsessed with the analysis of equilibria instead of with the paths leading from one equilibrium to the next (if an equilibrium existed in the first place).[29] The expectations of the economic agents and the ubiquitous uncertainty with respect to the future were absent in the Walrasian system.

Myrdal came back to the problem of dynamic method four years later, in the first sketch of what he during the 1930s would develop into what

[27] Ibid.

[28] Myrdal (1968, 1970a).

[29] Myrdal (1927).

eventually became *Monetary Equilibrium*.[30] There he set out to criticize Knut Wicksell's famous cumulative process, which spells out how an economy embarks on a path that leads away from equilibrium when the market rate of interest for some reason deviates from the natural or normal rate of interest (the rate that equates the demand for capital with the supply of savings) and sets off a process that changes the price level in a cumulative fashion. Myrdal criticized Wicksell for working with three different definitions of the latter interest rate and provided an extension of Wicksell's reasoning that incorporated anticipations with respect to the future. From that point, cumulative causation became a cornerstone in his own analysis.

Myrdal stressed the influence of the human factor in economic life in yet another way: in his investigation of the political element in economic theory.[31] This book, written in Swedish, was explicitly methodological. It attacked the mainstream of economic theory from the Enlightenment to Myrdal's own time, for hiding value premises behind a façade of purported objectivity. These value judgments were frequently far from innocent and biased the results of the investigations. Myrdal's solution to the problem was to make researchers state the value premises explicitly. He also provided guidelines for the choice of value premises that were to guide the research.

Gunnar Myrdal was directly involved in policy making in Sweden on several occasions. For him, this was an exercise in social engineering: an application of normative economics which hence had to rest on explicit value premises. Myrdal developed his views in a couple of programmatic articles in the early 1930s.[32] There, he made his ideological stance clear. Myrdal mistrusted the market. He advocated a fundamental reform of society based on planning. In order to reduce poverty and come to grips with social problems, the state had to intervene in the economy.

Just a few years later, in the mid-1930s, Myrdal got an opportunity to put his theories to test. He had prepared the ground by the publication of his book on the Swedish population problem together with Alva where they called for a complete overhaul of the Swedish welfare system and the creation of a society that built on solidarity through a

[30] Myrdal (1931a, 1933b, 1939).

[31] Myrdal (1930, 1953).

[32] Myrdal (1932a, b).

combination of social policy measures and income transfers from the rich to the poor. *Kris i befolkningsfrågan* became the starting point for what would become known as 'the Swedish model' of welfare policy. The book was widely debated in Sweden. Gunnar was drafted to the government Population Commission and became the driving force of it. The reports of the commission, in turn, constituted the first step in the creation of the modern welfare society in Sweden, a society that was based on strong government intervention with the market mechanism, measures to improve the lot of the low-income segments and income redistribution via the tax system.

During the writing of the population book and his work with practical social policy, Myrdal had gradually reached the insight that social engineering amounted to nothing but institutional reform. During his 1929–1930 visit to the United States, he had met some of the leading representatives of the American institutional school, without being impressed by their views. In the mid-1930s, however, he had begun to develop his own brand of institutionalism within a holistic approach to social science research. There were no purely economic, social or political problems, only problems which involved all aspects of society, variables which interacted and which were intimately related to the existing institutions which performed economic and social functions and determined the actions of the individual actors in the market.

With that, the stage was set for a major endeavor—Myrdal's best work—*An American Dilemma*. There, he pulled together all his methodological threads. Most important: he took a total view of American society. No aspect of the relations between whites and blacks escaped him when he formulated the racial problem in terms of the interaction between white prejudices and black living standards. At no time was his call for explicit value premises as important as then—in an environment full of preconceived notions of all kinds. Tackling the American racial problem amounted to a walk on eggshells. He emerged as victorious as ever Julius Caesar. His book was a huge success and contributed to major changes in the legislation on racial issues.

Myrdal next turned to the international aspects of poverty. During his tenure as executive secretary of the UN Economic Commission for Europe in Geneva, he had the energy to launch a major investigation of international inequality of incomes and living standards, an investigation which resulted in three books.[33] In these, Myrdal relates the issue of domestic inequalities to that of inequalities on the international level. He investigates how the progress of certain regions tends to generate backwash effects which serve to lower the living standards in other regions in a cumulative fashion and how the same mechanism operates on the international level. Instead of leading to factor price equalization, trade serves to set off cumulative effects which lead to increasing income disparities between nations.

The Geneva years also served to launch Myrdal's most grandiosely conceived research effort ever: his investigation of the causes of poverty in South Asia, notably India: *Asian Drama* and *The Challenge of World Poverty*, which presents the policy conclusions of the former work.[34] *Asian Drama* represents the culmination of Gunnar Myrdal's life-long methodological endeavor. There, as heterodox and institutional as ever, he pulls together all the threads that he had been spinning since the 1920s. Explicit value premises—'modernization ideals'—loom large. Mainstream development economics is subjected to devastating criticism, the importance of industrialization is played down and the role of labor utilization in agriculture is brought to the forefront, as is education, health and population aspects. Myrdal also remains true to his social engineering ideal. The importance of planning is stressed throughout and the problem of the 'soft' character of the South Asian state is analyzed at length.

As could be expected, Myrdal's analysis of the South Asian poverty problem provoked strong reactions from many quarters, in the West and in South Asia, from political conservatives, Soviet Marxist-Leninists and Western radicals alike, of course for different reasons. The conservatives reacted to his criticism of the market mechanism, the radicals objected to his professed aversion to Marxist economics and his failure to understand that underdevelopment in South Asia was the direct result of European colonialism, and the Asians blamed him for lack of familiarity with the on-the-ground reality of poverty and for his ethnocentric insistence of Western modernization ideals not shared by important segments of the

[33] Myrdal (1956a, b, 1957a).

[34] Myrdal (1968, 1970).

local societies. Virtually, all the critics agreed that the work was far too long.

More important, as subsequent events would show, however, Myrdal failed to predict the course of development of the economies of South Asia over the next few decades: the impressive progress made in terms of poverty eradication. Not least did he underestimate the power of foreign trade as a catalyst of economic change, the positive role of the state in a number of countries in the region and the advance made on the population front.

Asian Drama was Myrdal's last important scientific contribution. The last twenty years of his life were spent on a retrospective of what he had already accomplished. He kept coming back to his old themes in conferences and speeches. He revisited his two major works, *An American Dilemma* and *Asian Drama*; he stressed the importance of dealing with inequality and the moral aspects of the poverty problem. He also changed some of his former views, mainly those on foreign aid, which, he argued, had been largely inefficient and had better be concentrated on the poorest and distributed through non-governmental organizations like the Red Cross. Until the end of his life, however, Myrdal remained an optimist with respect to the future of mankind.

CHAPTER 2

Dynamics, Value Premises and Social Engineering

Dynamic Method: Price Formation and the Cumulative Process

In his doctoral dissertation from 1927, *Prisbildningsproblemet och föränderligheten* [*The Price Formation Problem and Economic Change*],[1] Gunnar Myrdal attempted to extend the static neoclassical price theory. He was inspired by the formulation provided by his teacher, Gustav Cassel, who considered prices to be established by the interaction of three factors: demand, the technical conditions of production and the available means of production.[2] Cassel was also concerned with the dynamics of price formation, through the influence of such exogenous factors as population growth on the three 'immediate' determinants, but never incorporated it into any explicit analysis.[3]

Myrdal took upon himself to fill the void 'to a certain extent',[4] by working expectations with respect to the future into the analysis of price formation. '... the price formation takes place in human minds. Thus, notions of the degree of probability of future changes and in addition

[1] Myrdal (1927).

[2] Cassel (1923, p. 152).

[3] Hansson (1982, pp. 30–32).

[4] Myrdal (1927, p. 4).

M. Lundahl, *The Dynamics of Poverty*, Palgrave Studies in the History of Economic Thought,
https://doi.org/10.1007/978-3-030-73347-6_2

valuations of the very moment of uncertainty in these notions will exert an influence on price formation at the present time'.[5] To this, he added the existence of time lags in the reaction of the allocation of production factors to changes in demand and supply—'stickiness'—and risk. The interaction between the present and the future, as Myrdal saw it, worked in two directions:

> The dynamic price formation gives rise to two completely different problems, which must be strictly separated. One problem is how one price situation is transformed into another. The question deals with the causal effects of the actually realized changes *forwards in time*. The changes, however, also have effects *backwards in time*, since they are anticipated. It is the latter problem which is the primary one from the theoretical point of view. Because it is this price formation situation, where the anticipations have contributed to the outcome, which is hit by the changes and which then develops into a new one. The investigation of the former problem in other words requires that the latter problem is solved.[6]

In other words, Myrdal's problem was 'how equilibrium values and prices are determined in a world in which expectations form part of the data upon which decisions are taken'.[7]

We will stop here. This is not the place to go into the details of Myrdal's analysis of the price formation process. We simply note that from the very beginning of his academic career he was concerned with dynamic, as opposed to static, analysis.

Wicksell's Cumulative Process

Four years after his thesis defense, Myrdal was to extend his insistence on dynamics into the use of cumulative causation. The occasion was his critique and extension of a mechanism introduced by Knut Wicksell: his cumulative process, the process which sets off upward or downward movements in the price level. In his original formulation, he took as his point of departure what he called the natural rate of interest. It was introduced in *Interest and Prices*:

[5] Ibid., p. 8.

[6] Ibid., p. 21.

[7] Seccareccia (1992, p. 154).

> There is a certain rate of interest which is neutral with respect to commodity prices, and tends neither to raise nor to lower them. This is necessarily the same as the rate of interest which would be determined by supply and demand if no use were made of money and all lending would be effected in the form of real capital goods. It comes to much the same thing as the current value of the *natural interest on capital.*[8]

In the second volume of his *Lectures on Political Economy*,[9] Wicksell changed his definition: 'The rate of interest at which *the demand for loan capital and the supply of savings* exactly agree, and which more or less corresponds to the expected yield on the newly created capital, will ... be the normal or natural real rate'.[10] According to Wicksell, there is no reason why we should expect the normal or natural rate of interest to coincide with the bank lending rate. If banks lend at an interest rate which diverges from the natural one, the price level will change. Suppose that the lending rate of interest falls below the normal rate. Then, producers benefit from lending and will expand their production and investment. This will in turn expand the demand for goods and services used for investment and set off a process where the price level will increase.

Wicksell saw the process as a cumulative one: 'It is ... frequently the case that quite a small fall in the [lending] rate of interest would *immediately* bring about a much greater rise in prices. The price which can be paid for goods obtained by means of credit is higher the longer the period during which the credit is utilized'.[11] (In the case of an increased lending rate, producers will make losses and be discouraged from investing, etc.) Carl Uhr explains the logic in his *Economic Doctrines of Knut Wicksell*:

> In fact, if the process is of long duration, it may accelerate in its later stages, or, as he put it, 'create its own draft.' This would happen if entrepreneurs (who are usually assumed to make decisions for the future on the expectation of the continuation of current prices), after having experienced some rounds of price increases, begin to make their decisions on expectations of increasing prices. In such cases speculation is aroused and prices may reach great heights. The process itself may then terminate in a crisis

[8] Wicksell (1936, p. 10). German original: Wicksell (1898).

[9] Swedish original: Wicksell (1906).

[10] Wicksell (1935, p. 193).

[11] Wicksell (1936, p. 91).

> as increasing production maladjustments, overextension of investment in various branches of the economy, etc., engender doubts concerning the continuation of further price increases.[12]

Alternatively, the banks (sluggishly) adjust their lending rates or some exogenous change brings an end to the process.

Myrdal's Adaptation

Knut Wicksell's idea of cumulative causation was picked up, criticized, extended and brought to bear on completely different issues by Gunnar Myrdal from the 1930s to the 1970s. Myrdal began with an immanent critique of Wicksell, developed gradually in a Swedish, a German, and, finally, an English version of what in the end became *Monetary Equilibrium*.[13] By immanent critique, he meant a critique which, based on Wicksell's assumptions examined the internal consistency of his reasoning. He focused on Wicksell's central notion: the normal rate of interest. Myrdal took issue with the fact that Wicksell had chosen to define monetary equilibrium in a threefold way. The normal rate of interest coincides with the lending rate and at the same time equates savings and investment and ensures that the price level remains constant. Myrdal discussed whether these three conditions are compatible with each other. He argued that Wicksell's analysis was too simplified, that—in the same way as with price formation—it is necessary to include anticipations in the reasoning and that the analysis must be carried out in the context of a monetary economy.

More interesting than Myrdal's criticism, from the present point of view, however, is the fact that he accepted Wicksell's notion of a cumulative process:

> On one point … Myrdal absorbed Wicksell without significant modification, namely the conception of a 'cumulative process.' With respect to the problem at hand, this could be defined as a '*dynamic deviation in one direction or the other from a monetary equilibrium.*' And he added that 'the essential feature of the process is a shift in production which brings with it an increased production of real capital if the dynamic process has an

[12] Uhr (1962, p. 233).

[13] Myrdal (1931a, 1933b, 1939).

upward direction and a decreased production if the process has a downward trend.'[14]

Gunnar Myrdal was to extend the into cumulative process circular causation as well and make use of the principle in his later works. We will come back to this.

The Problem of Value Premises

Already before Myrdal took issue with Wicksell's formulation of the cumulative process, he had begun to develop his third pillar, the one dealing with value premises. In 1930, he published *Vetenskap och politik i nationalekonomien* [English translation, *The Political Element in the Development of Economic Theory*, 1953].[15] In this book, 'one of the most famous methodological treatises in economics',[16] Myrdal attacked his colleagues for posing as objective scientists in situations where they were in fact spreading value-laden political statements which lacked a solid scientific foundation, using them to formulate economic policies. They erroneously assumed that their policy recommendations were based on theories only. In the preface to the second edition of his book, he notes that 'the book had its origin in the intention to write a popular polemical pamphlet against the careless and erroneous way of the older [Swedish] generation to present political views as scientific conclusions', but that in the end he became so fascinated by his topic that he chose to 'plunge deeply into the big methodological problem and soon forgot about the native country and its petty conflicts'.[17]

In his writing of *Vetenskap och politik*, Myrdal was inspired by the philosopher Axel Hägerström, the leading member of the Uppsala School of Philosophy, who was a sworn enemy of everything that reeked of metaphysics and known, especially to his critics, to be a 'value nihilist'

[14] Barber (2008, p. 26). The two quotations are from Myrdal (1939, pp. 29 and 34), respectively.

[15] Myrdal (1930, 1953). The story of how the book was written is told in Swedberg (1990).

[16] Velupillai (1992, p. 137).

[17] Myrdal (1972, pp. 7–8).

who argued that no objective values existed.[18] Many years later, in the Postscript to *Value in Social Theory*, Myrdal acknowledged his debt of gratitude, describing his years as a law student at Stockholm College:

> ... two or three amongst us felt ... the strong positive stimulus from the remarkable Uppsala philosopher, Professor Axel Hägerström (1869–1939) ... His major works were devoted to a critique of the notions, concepts and methods of reasoning in jurisprudence, which he showed to be self-contradictory, false or meaningless. With the aid of much learning he traced their origin to primitive magic in prehistoric times, from which stems also our prevailing tendency to conceptualize. These works are rather forbidding and were not studied thoroughly by any of us. But in some more general writings and in his personal teaching, which in the 'twenties reverberated among the young intellectuals in Sweden far beyond Uppsala, he clearly and strikingly expressed the importance of drawing a line between beliefs about reality and valuations of it. The two are not on the same logical level, for beliefs can, valuations cannot, be judged by the criteria of true and false.[19]

Positive and Normative Economics

Vetenskap och politik is an essay in the history of economic ideas. Myrdal investigated the development of the mainstream of economics from the Enlightenment to his own time, uncovering the underlying assumptions and the value judgments and political speculation—elements that were seldom spelled out explicitly or discussed. 'We must look upon the majority of modern economic doctrines as modified reminiscences of very old political thinking, conceived in days when a teleological meaning and a normative purpose were more openly part of the subject-matter of economics',[20] he wrote.

Not that he condemned normative economics: 'There is ... wide agreement', argued Myrdal, 'that economics ought to be "practical"'.[21] It is to a large extent an instrumental science and Myrdal wanted to construct a

[18] Hägerström, who was not well-known outside Sweden, was introduced to an international audience by Ernst Cassirer (1939). See also Wallner (1961), Nordin (1983), and Källström (1986).

[19] Myrdal (1958, p. 250).

[20] Myrdal (1953, p. x).

[21] Ibid., p. 191.

'technology of economics' that could be of help when it came to deigning policy interventions. The question rather was how this could be achieved. Actual practice left a lot to be desired:

> ... the economic reasoning is often obscured by the fact that normative concepts are not introduced explicitly, but in the shape of general 'concepts'. [...] All definitions are tools which we construct in order to observe and analyse reality. They are 'instrumental' and have no justification in their own right. By operating with definitions which purport to be universally valid, people have often succeeded in making an implied political principle appear logically 'correct'. Psychologically, it is the other way round. The emotive force which is rationalized in the implied principle makes the normative element that has been disguised in the definition appear to be absolute and 'correct'. The perpetual hide-and-seek in economics consists in concealing the norm in the concept. It is thus imperative to eradicate not only the explicit principles but above all the valuations tacitly implied by the basic concepts. Being concealed, they are more insidious and more elusive, and hence more likely to breed confusion.[22]

As Erik Ljungar has pointed out, in 1930, Myrdal still thought that objectivity was possible to some extent, in economic research.[23] 'Economists are on safe ground as long as they describe actual events and their causal connections, and as long as they examine the effects of certain clearly defined "interventions" under specified conditions',[24] that is, as long as they work within what is conventionally known as 'positive' economics. Once we move into the field of normative recommendations, however, severe complications arise. For economics to become what Myrdal chose to call a practical 'technology' due attention must be paid to the influence of the institutions in society. These institutions of society are not given, however, but possible to change. However, in order to determine which changes are feasible the distribution of power among social groups must be mapped.

> The technology of economics should reflect possible strategies in a 'war game'. It would be of practical importance if it throws light on the possible course of future developments and probable trends. It could also be used

[22] Ibid., p. 192.

[23] Ljungar (1999, p. 44).

[24] Myrdal (1953, p. 198).

> to clarify the relation between various programmes and the interests of the groups which sponsor them.
>
> Certain policies may thus seem to be ill-conceived or doomed to failure from the start. In this way political intentions could be clarified and orientated. Such a study of the politics of economics could claim to be objective, just because it makes no recommendations save those which follow some specified, clearly expressed interest. For the same reason, it could not yield absolutely valid conclusions in the sense of postulates of an economically correct conduct as such, except, possibly, in the limited sphere where interests can be shown to be identical.[25]

The solution of the normative problem, according to Myrdal of 1930, was to bring the value premises that govern policy decisions out in the open. The technology of economics 'should always formulate its value premises explicitly in concrete terms and relate them to the actual valuations of social groups'.[26]

A Change of Position

Myrdal would soon change his views. When writing the preface to the second edition of *Vetenskap och politik*, in 1972, he claimed to have been methodologically naïve when he wrote the first edition:

> I then still thought that there was an economics free of valuations, and this shows throughout the book. Now I know, after continued study of many areas, that this opinion is erroneous and that value premises are necessary already when it comes to observing reality, establish the facts and the causal relations between facts.[27]

In his inaugural lecture for the Lars Hierta chair in Economics and Finance, on *The Changing World View in Economics*, in 1935, in the middle of the Great Depression, Myrdal took his views on explicit value premises one step further. There he argued that the world was experiencing 'one of the great and decisive times of unrest for the entire social science as well as for social life' in general, and that this glaringly exposed the fact that research necessarily rested on a world view, which,

[25] Ibid.

[26] Ibid., p. 204.

[27] Myrdal (1972, p. 13).

since the problems dealt with belonged to the field of social science, also encompassed a philosophy of life. 'The world view determines the questions to be dealt with on the theoretical level, and the philosophy of life determines the value premises on the practical level'.[28]

There was no way to escape the aprioristic, even on the theoretical level. Biases would creep as much into positive economics as into normative investigations. The problem was that in order to receive an answer you must pose a question, but the question was a result of a choice which thus to a certain extent determined the answer. 'The answer is hence not, and cannot be, unbiased'.[29] The problem of the social sciences was that they were intimately related to the changes that were taking place in the world economy and society. They could never aspire to discover any 'constants'. 'The objects and subjects of [social] research cannot be isolated from one another. Man is the measure of everything; within the social sciences the very view hence moves in relation to the movement of the object viewed'.[30] Myrdal cautioned against the 'scientifically naïve', uncritical acceptance of conventional worldviews and philosophies of life, which—without reflection—are seen as 'natural'. The superior alternative was to work with an explicit set of value premises—a conviction that permeated all his subsequent scientific work. As Kurt Dopfer puts it,

> Economists anticipate their ideological intentions; their choices of problem areas and explanatory variables are inevitably colored by those anticipations. Myrdal criticized economists for their deliberate concealment of value judgments, and argued that ideological preferences and value judgments should be stated *explicitly* and openly.[31]

The Choice of Value Premises

These value premises must be chosen consciously and methodically, in such a way as to be relevant for important groups in society:

> … the best tradition of political economy … has always aimed at social policy. [The technology of economics, however], would have to become

[28] Myrdal (1935a, p. 8).

[29] Ibid., p. 9.

[30] Ibid., p. 13.

[31] Dopfer (1988, p. 229).

> more relativistic, i.e. it would have to be related to *explicit and concrete value premises*. If this science of economic politics, after thus having been made conditional and relativistic, is to have any practical significance, the chosen value premises must express the interests of all the strong social groups. This requires an analysis of the field of social interests. But the crucial problem is to discover these interests, while taking account of all the institutions which are feasible under political pressure.[32]

In an opening address to the British Sociological Association in 1953, Myrdal came back to his insistence on a conscious and coherent set of explicit value premises: 'They cannot be *a priori* self-evident or generally valid. They should be chosen, but not arbitrarily, for the choice must meet the criteria of relevance and significance to the society we live in'.[33] For a premise to be relevant, it must correspond to 'the interests and ideals of actual persons and groups of persons'. Significance, in turn, refers to 'valuations which are held by substantial groups of people or by small groups with substantial social power'. However, nothing forbids the analyst to select other values. The value premises must also be consistent, i.e., free from contradictions.[34]

The conscious and rational selection of value premises constitutes the foundation upon which policy formulation must rest. 'When the value premise is chosen and defined, it will, in combination with the analysis of facts, permit rational policy conclusions. These conclusions are rational because they are … hypothetical. They only spell out the logical policy implications of the selected value premise in a known context of reality'.[35]

It is only under these circumstances that it is possible to arrive at rational economic policy making based on feasible goals:

> Only if economists are modest in their claims and renounce all pretensions to postulate universal laws and norms can they promote effectively their practical objectives, viz., to keep political arguments rational, that is to say,

[32] Myrdal (1953, p. 199).

[33] Myrdal (1958, p. 52).

[34] Ibid., pp. 157, 158.

[35] Ibid., pp. 48–49. For a critical examination of Myrdal's argumentation, see Rosier (1992).

> to base them on as complete and as correct a knowledge of the facts as possible.[36]

Value Premises Revisited

Gunnar Myrdal came back to the issue of value premises in a small book in 1969.[37] He pointed out that the ethos of social science is the search for 'objective' truth and then focused on possible sources of bias in social science research and how to avoid them:

> The most fundamental problems facing the social scientist are … what is objectivity, and how can the student of social problems liberate himself from (1) the powerful heritage of earlier writings in his field of inquiry, ordinarily containing normative and teleological notions inherited from past generations and founded upon the metaphysical philosophies of natural law and utilitarianism from which all our social and economic theories have branched off; (2) the influences of the entire cultural, social, economic, and political milieu of the society where he lives, works, and earns his living and his status; and (3) the influence stemming from his own personality, as molded not only by traditions and environment, but also by his individual history, constitution, and inclinations?[38]

Myrdal did not stop there, however, but also raised the issue of how to reconcile objectivity with the desire to change society—the quest for social engineering that we will come back to below. 'How can the search for true knowledge be combined with moral and political valuations? How can truth be related to ideals?'[39] As always, the solution was to make the researcher's value premises explicit and choose them in a systematic way:

> … the logical means available for protecting ourselves from biases are broadly these: to raise the valuations actually determining our theoretical as well as our practical research to full awareness, to scrutinize them from the point of view of relevance, significance, and feasibility in the society under study, to transform them into specific value premises for research,

[36] Myrdal (1953, p. 206).

[37] Myrdal (1969).

[38] Ibid., pp. 3–4.

[39] Ibid., p. 4.

> and to determine approach and define concepts in terms of a set of value premises which have been explicitly stated.[40]

The method chosen by Myrdal has important consequences for economic analysis:

> One important consequence of Myrdal's approach derives from his claim that the social sciences are fundamentally characterized by value judgments at all levels, from the theoretical frameworks and the concepts employed to the factual choices required to test such theories. Accepting that values do play such a role leads us to conclude that it is impossible to distinguish clearly ends from means, or positive economics from normative economics. This is not, however, a condition that we can try to avoid, since it constitutes part of the very essence of any social science. It is thus utopian to believe in a value-free political economy.[41]

As Myrdal himself expressed it, 'It is true that, in principle, all scientific work has to be based on value premises. There is no view without a viewpoint, no answers except to questions. In the viewpoint applied and the questions raised, valuations are involved'.[42]

* * *

Vetenskap och politik was a book that aggravated conventional economists. In Sweden, Gustav Cassel swore never to read it, and Eli Heckscher, who, like Cassel, had been one of the targets for Myrdal's attack when he presented his ideas to the Political Economy Club in Stockholm in January 1928, and who was conflict-prone, hated it and talked about it as a treason of science.[43] When the book was published in German in 1932 and English in 1953, it irritated both radicals and middle-of-the-road economists.

Richard Swedberg summarized the state of the art in 1990:

[40] Ibid., p. 5.

[41] Peltier (1992, p. 188).

[42] Myrdal (1974, p. 147).

[43] Swedberg (1990, p. xxi).

Over the years, Myrdal's book has been much discussed. The general verdict is that the book is excellent in its genre. But *The Political Element* has also hit several sore spots. Soviet economists, for example, do not like the book, especially the part containing the critique of the labor theory of value. And many mainstream economics have been irritated by Myrdal's work as well. To Edward S. Mason, *The Political Element* was 'unduly critical'. Fritz Machlup said it contains 'gratuitous and misleading' remarks about the need for analytical abstractions. And for Ludwig von Mises, Myrdal's book was 'already outdated at the time of its first publication in Sweden,' since Schmoller and the institutionalists had made the same critique many years earlier. To John Hicks, *The Political Element* was 'a *reductio ad absurdum*.' Once Myrdal had stopped wielding his axe, Hicks said, economics 'lies flat'. Finally, the kind of irritation that many economists apparently have felt when reading Myrdal's book comes to a particularly clear expression in Mark Blaug's standard work, *Economic Theory in Retrospect*. Blaug here speaks of "Myrdal-type books," by which he means the kind of books which say that economics is useless. [...] mainstream economics is still smarting from Myrdal's youthful whipping in 1930'.[44]

The Active State

The fourth pillar in Myrdal's approach to the poverty problem was his strong belief in politically motivated public intervention in the economy and social engineering—engineering that rested on explicit value premises:

> In ... [Myrdal's] life intensely theoretical periods alternated without interruption with periods of equally intense practical political activity. During the 1930s, these two aspects were merged into the extensive and frantic activity that ... [Myrdal] and his wife Alva unfolded in order to sketch the outlines of a new social policy, which was to differ from both the traditional liberal and the traditional socialist social policy. In comparison to the former, the new social policy would exceed the help to make people help themselves and include democratically decided redistribution of the fruits of production as a civic right. In comparison to the latter, it would bridge

[44] Ibid., p. xxii. The quotations are from Mason (1934), Machlup (1955), von Mises (1954), Hicks (1954) and Blaug (1978).

> the gap between day-to-day programs and long-run goals through a technical and practical orientation towards social problems and hence renew the reformist socialism.[45]

In *Vetenskap och politik i nationalekonomien* Myrdal spoke of a 'technology of economics'. In the English version of the book, he explained what he meant: 'a scientific theory of how policy can serve concrete interests'.[46]

> Only the theory of price formation and distribution would have to be reformulated from this particular point of view. The theory would, as it were, have to be turned around. Instead of answering how, in given conditions, prices, incomes, and other quantities are determined, the theory ought to be able to answer the question what interferences, if any would be in the interest of what groups.[47]

The 'technology of economics' that Myrdal had in mind would, however, not necessarily be accepted by the decision makers. In a lecture held at Harvard more than forty years later, he compared the natural and the social sciences. Whereas the findings of the former were easy to apply and were welcomed by companies and governments, the situation of the latter was completely different:

> Our discoveries and inventions in the social field must generally be applied by the collectivities, i.e., in the first place, the state and subordinated communities. They must become public policies, accepted by those who have the power to determine action or inaction by those collectivities. Ordinarily, these people – from the elected or appointed officials down to the members of the electorates – have their preconceived ideas. No less ordinarily, these ideas are founded upon what they feel to be their interests. They may be short-sightedly or even erroneously conceived, aside from the fact that they do not necessarily, or even commonly, coincide with what would emerge as the public interest of the citizenry, if they were all alert and rational.[48]

[45] Gustafsson (1987–1989, p. 152).

[46] Myrdal (1953, p. 196).

[47] Ibid.

[48] Myrdal (1974, pp. 154–55).

The ruling constellations were not given once and for all, however. The new price theory that Myrdal discussed in *Vetenskap och politik* did not take the institutional setting for granted the way conventional analysis did:

> The real difficulty of constructing a technology of economics in this sense would be that we are not entitled to take the existing institutional set-up for granted. By institutional set-up is meant the legal order, and the customs, habits, and conventions, which are sanctioned, or at least tolerated, by that legal order. A purely theoretical analysis of price formation can and, indeed, always has abstracted from institutional changes.[49]

The actual political struggle was very much about the institutional setting and short-term political constellations were likely to differ substantially from long-run constellations. Myrdal hence called for the inclusion of institutional change into the economic analysis. 'An inquiry into economic interests should therefore treat the whole institutional set-up as a variable. It should also examine to what extent any groups are sufficiently powerful to bring about institutional changes throughout the price system'.[50]

A Programmatic Article

In 1929, Gunnar and Alva Myrdal both received Rockefeller Foundation fellowships to go to the United States during the academic year 1929–1930. They arrived in New York in mid-October 1929, just before Black Thursday, the 29th, the beginning of the stock market crash that marked the onset of the Great Depression. What they saw was something that would stay with them for the rest of their lives: abject poverty and extreme inequality:

> … they … witnessed the country's economy nearing collapse and the whole world shaken as a result, all while Herbert Hoover's government stood powerless to reverse the process.
>
> It was in the United States, as a result, that Alva and Gunnar Myrdal claimed to have wakened up politically. Even apart from the Depression,

[49] Myrdal (1953, p. 196).

[50] Ibid., pp. 196–97.

> they were profoundly shaken by the brutal contrasts between millionaires and slum dwellers that they now witnessed. In Sweden, there was already greater equality and local communities along with government agencies had long provided support for those in need. To see such great poverty and such injustice toward racial and religious minorities radicalized both of them. Earlier they had been more preoccupied with their studies and their plans for the future and above all with one another than with social conditions at home or abroad. Neither the aftershocks following the Great War, nor the battles for women's suffrage in Sweden and in so many nations had touched them as conditions in America did now.[51]

Their US experience would soon be converted into a call for action on the home front. In 1932, the year when he joined the Social Democratic Party, which won the elections that year, Gunnar Myrdal published a programmatic article in two parts: 'Socialpolitikens dilemma [The Dilemma of Social Policy]'.[52] There he sketched the history of social policy in Sweden since the late nineteenth century and its evolution into 'an entire ideology which to a certain extent managed to ... more or less join a liberal conservatism and social reforms'.[53] After the First World War, practical social policy had developed considerably. It had created a bureaucracy, and in all ways commanded respect. But, argued Myrdal, the very ideology behind it was showing signs of consumption. Swedish social policy fit neither the liberal nor the socialist ideology. It was a product of a merger of the two—a compromise. The socialists had become reformist and the liberals had moved toward the left.

In spite of this, Myrdal discerned an opening rift between the two ideologies. The very expansion of the scope of social policy served to create increasing expectations with respect to its results.

> Little by little, we have all adopted certain moral demands which are difficult to get away from. Nobody must starve or be in want of any kind. The sick should have ideal care without any real expense on their own part. All children should have the same chances in life, something which does not materialize just through free schooling. Each family should have a dwelling fit for human beings which makes it possible for the home to provide a reasonably good organization of the leisure of the members of the family

[51] Bok (1992, p. 7).

[52] Myrdal (1932a, b).

[53] Myrdal (1932a, p. 2).

> … Our idea about what is luxury is being steadily revised downward: ever more expense items are placed within the frame of the 'necessities' and 'quasi-necessities' of the classical economists. Everybody has a '*right*' to a standard of living which is adequate for human beings, one which is put higher and higher. Yes, everybody 'actually' has a right to live *equally* well: the income and wealth situation is … actually ever more seen as an 'arbitrary work of man'; and completely in line with the development of the liberal economy, social policy is beginning to be seen precisely in this light. – Do you feel how the philosophy of equality of the Enlightenment is in earnest penetrating everybody's way of looking at things? Social policy itself has conveyed an ideology that uninterruptedly increases the demands on the results of social policy.[54]

Myrdal felt that the increasing demand for decent housing among the urban and rural poor would trigger a class conflict of interest—precisely the conflict that social policy was supposed to defuse. As social policy progressed from an assistance provided by 'society', founded on 'authoritative benevolence and a sense of righteousness',[55] to a more general redistribution of the fruits of production enforced through the democratic machinery precisely by the groups that stood to gain from it, it would become ever more difficult to maintain the common ideology. While the liberal ideology had no difficulty accepting a more equal distribution of incomes on the theoretical level, once it came to *actual* redistribution, the conflict of interest would be uncovered. According to the liberal ideology, the assistance had to be given on such conditions that it did not decrease the willingness of the individuals to come to grips with their situation by themselves. This was the dilemma of social policy as viewed from the liberal camp.

The socialist ideology with respect to social policy was facing a dilemma as well. Social policy had been substituted for more radical[56] redistribution measures with respect to production and property. Myrdal saw 'a risk that the workers would begin to regard social policy as mere patches on the rags, and that they would again turn their attention to more

[54] Myrdal (1932b, pp. 14–15).

[55] Ibid., p. 15.

[56] After their 1929–1930 visit to the United States, Gunnar and Alva Myrdal 'begin to use the term "radical" and refer to "tradition" as a synonym of "backwardness" or "hostility to progress"' (Etzemüller, 2014, p. 54).

radical change – a change of the "system."'[57] He pointed out that social policy in Sweden hitherto had dealt exclusively with symptoms. 'We give poor relief to the poor, unemployment compensation to the unemployed, put the sick into hospitals, detain the alcoholics in detoxification centers, lunatics in madhouses, etc. but do very little to prevent the emergence of these phenomena'.[58] This, he stated, had made the experts on social policy demand a more or less radical prophylactic social policy for several decades—a policy which would save both the individual and society from future costs.

The new ideology was not based on sentimentality but was 'intellectualistic and cooly rationalistic'. It was divested of 'the liberalistic idea brakes'. It was down to earth. 'Its romanticism is that of the engineer'.[59] Its technical calculations were brave and abstract. It was even a bit inhuman. Myrdal saw a new ideology spring from the technically oriented discussion of social policy: 'It is radical in the sense that it calmly presupposes very deep-going reforms of the social "system", which is hence no longer respected as the foundation of the "reforms", since the reforms to a large extent are directed toward the change of precisely this foundation'.[60]

Myrdal considered the new approach to social policy to be a possible ingredient of the renewal of the reformistic socialism. The new approach rested on planning, not a far-fetched idea, he argued, since planning was increasingly accepted even by the business community—the 'trustification' of companies and the organization of the markets for dairy products along monopolistic cooperative lines. Planning was no longer taboo. In his 1935 inaugural lecture, Myrdal pointed out that the incentives for planning came from traditions both on the right and the left.[61] 'Economic planning means that you are prepared to push the measures far enough for them to have maximum efficiency, whichever the measures happen to be and regardless of their purpose. The more radical social policy is precisely the planned economy variety of social

[57] Myrdal (1932b, p. 21).

[58] Ibid., p. 24.

[59] Ibid., p. 25.

[60] Ibid., p. 28.

[61] Myrdal (1935a, p. 14).

policy'.[62] As Myrdal told James Angresano in 1980, 'Planning is changing institutions'.[63]

Gunnar Myrdal did not trust the ability of the unregulated market to maximize efficiency and welfare in society. In his inaugural lecture, he described the attitude of the advocates of a planned economy:

> ... all varieties of planning endeavors are based on the need for a central direction of the economy. You don't trust the private initiative, the responsibility of the individual and the interaction of the free powers. You demand deep-going interventions. These interventions are furthermore directed toward the very 'system', on production and exchange, the monetary and credit system, that is those parts of the price formation that liberalism in principle wanted to keep free from interventions.[64]

Myrdal considered the liberal market economy to be a static, unrealistic construction, while the planning advocates professed a dynamic, realistic view of society and its institutions. Planning was a necessity:

> At the bottom of the formation of social views ... the paradox of unemployment is gnawing: on the one hand misery and hardships, on the other hand an abundance of goods, badly utilized labor and unused capital resources – plenty of wheat and no bread. This paradox is directed like an accusation toward the very system of production and not just the distribution system. Because it formulates the economic policy problem as a problem of organization, a problem of economic planning.[65]

For both Gunnar and Alva Myrdal, the 1930s became a decade of practical application of the new—social engineering—approach to social policy. Gunnar could 'put into practice the technology of economics that he had advocated in Vetenskap och politik i nationalekonomien', writes Bo Gustafsson.[66] He was convinced that experts had an important role to play in the formulation of economic and social policy, and little by little, he became directly involved in interventionist policy himself. He

[62] Myrdal (1932b, pp. 30–31).

[63] Angresano (1997, p. 159).

[64] Myrdal (1932b, p. 19).

[65] Myrdal (1935a, p. 34).

[66] Gustafsson (1987–1989, p. 149).

was elected to the First Chamber of the Swedish parliament in 1936 for the Social Democrats, but even more important is that he was called upon as an expert in official government commissions on fiscal policy, population, agriculture and social policy. His 'most important achievements in this context consisted in his contributions to the new economic policy and welfare policy'.[67]

Monetary and Fiscal Policy

Already the year before the publication of 'Socialpolitikens dilemma', 1931, in the book *Sveriges väg genom penningkrisen* [Sweden's Road through the Monetary Crisis],[68] Myrdal stressed the importance of a monetary policy 'that is *possible* given the actual circumstances and *desirable* from the point of view of the economic interests and the political views of different groups of citizens'.[69] The monetary issue formed part of 'our general fiscal, economic and social policy'.[70] The feasibility and efficiency of the monetary policy was dependent on the measures undertaken in these other fields. Most important of all was to increase production, 'the branch on which we are all sitting'.[71] The welfare of the Swedes rested on that, and Myrdal argued that in order to preserve and develop 'the democratic and private capitalist character sector of the Swedish economy' and preserve the smooth function of the system of checks and balances in Swedish society a measure of planned economy had to be added, at least for the time being.[72]

In March 1932, Myrdal was appointed to the official Committee on Unemployment [Arbetslöshetskommissionen] which had been working since 1927. The following year, he was asked by the Social Democratic Minister of Finance Ernst Wigforss to produce a memorandum endorsing the use of an expansionist fiscal policy to combat unemployment.[73] This memorandum, which became the theoretical foundation of

[67] Ibid.

[68] Myrdal (1931b).

[69] Ibid., p. 9.

[70] Ibid., p. 21.

[71] Ibid., p. 94.

[72] Ibid., p. 127.

[73] Myrdal (1933a).

an active government policy, and which was appended to the 1933 budget and finance bill, advocated the use of public works as a countercyclical measure—to make use of the otherwise unemployed, stimulate production and increase government revenues. Public works were superior to mere relief payments from both the economic and the social policy point of view:

> Public works, in contrast to relief payments, result in increased production. Their stimulating effect on the economy is more powerful and to a larger extent directed towards the capital goods producing industries badly hit by the depression. And the effects on the moral and future production capacity of the workers are generally more favorable. It is only when the scope for public works is exhausted that relief payments for those still unemployed are motivated.[74]

The following year, he extended his reasoning in *Finanspolitikens ekonomiska verkningar* [The Economic Effects of Fiscal Policy], published as an appendix to the main report of the Committee on Unemployment. There he also stressed the interventionist nature of economic policy measures:

> ... public finance [offentlig hushållning] – together with all other public activities – constitutes a part of the institutional framework of the market economy and hence one of its essential conditions. By changing this condition, you can change the actual process of market price formation and its results. Herein lies *the necessarily political character of public finance.*[75]

Myrdal's reasoning rested on the social engineering perspective. The goal of public economic policy was to change the process of price formation in such a way as to make it meet public goals by changing the institutional framework within which the private sector had to work. Public finance differed fundamentally from private business. While the latter was based on principles of profitability, the former was not. In the public finance context revenues were a function of the desired expenditures, and the latter were in turn determined by their economic and social consequences, and these had nothing to do with profitability. On the contrary, as Bo

[74] Ibid., p. 75.

[75] Myrdal (1934, p. 14).

Gustafsson explains, 'Most of the ordinary direct expenditures for, among other things, education, research, social care, above all of youths, unemployment and assistance in times of crisis, are of importance for the future and in certain cases only for the future'.[76]

[76] Gustafsson (1987–1989, p. 151).

CHAPTER 3

Social Engineering in Practice: The Population Issue

Gunnar Myrdal's interest in methodological issues predated his interest in poverty, but gradually, during the 1930s, he began to produce works which dealt not only with economic policy but which in one way or the other touched social problems directly. Myrdal had become interested in demographic issues in the late 1920s,[1] not least in connection with his work on the political element in economics, but he had not yet made the direct connection with social policy. The first work of this kind was a book written together with his wife, Alva, which would later be questioned because of its references to the theories of race biology and race hygiene in vogue at the time when it was published, in 1934.[2]

[1] See Carlson (1990, pp. 40–42) for details.

[2] Gunnar and Alva Myrdal shared a life-long intellectual, fertile and crossbreeding companionship. This has been the subject of several studies, e.g., Hertz (1971), Lindskog (1981), Bok (1987), Carlson (1990), Fölster (1992), Nilsson (1994), Åkerman (1997), Vinterhed (2003), Hederberg (2004), Gröning (2006), Hirdman (2006, 2011), and Etzemüller (2014). For a subjective evaluation of the quality of some of these works, see Etzemüller (2014, p. 15). For an even more subjective view of the couple, see the books by their son Jan Myrdal (1968, Swedish translation 1983, 1982, 1984, 1993, 1994, 1998, 2002, 2019) which deal with his childhood and adolescence. For a discussion of whether these books should rightly be considered fiction or autobiography, see Cervin (1997).

M. Lundahl, *The Dynamics of Poverty*, Palgrave Studies in the History of Economic Thought,
https://doi.org/10.1007/978-3-030-73347-6_3

Crisis

The cooperation with Alva was the most important intellectual partnership in the life of Gunnar Myrdal:

> His belief in the power of analysis and rational criticism to bring about change for the better was rooted in his earliest adoption of an Enlightenment world-view and reinforced by Alva Myrdal's egalitarian and humane ideals. All who knew Alva and Gunnar Myrdal could feel the force of this shared and mutually reinforcing foundation for their activities. [...] In Alva, Gunnar found someone with a similar belief that progress was possible but with more clearly delineated ideals and a passion to put them into practice.[3]

In their book, with the slightly funny title *Kris i befolkningsfrågan* [Crisis in the Population Question],[4] as their daughter Sissela Bok puts it, the Myrdals '[stole] a conservative issue for radical purposes ... [arguing] that only sweeping social reform could raise fertility rates and thereby prevent the gradual disappearance of the Swedish people'.[5] They took issue with the neo-Malthusian ideas of the 1880s which held that Sweden was overpopulated. In fact, they contended, the problem was the opposite. Birth and population growth rates were 'catastrophically' low in Sweden,[6] although not uniformly so. The poor kept breeding too large families while middle-class people actively reduced their fertility. Altogether, however, in order to keep the population at a stationary level, 40 percent more births were required. If nothing was done, the country ran the risk of embarking upon the journey to extinction of the Swedish population. Immigration was no solution, since the immigrants were likely to come from far away, including from Asia and Africa. They would be difficult to assimilate and would pose problems for the labor movement. Unemployment was higher than ever, in the middle of the depression. Catastrophe was lurking around the corner.[7]

[3] Bok (1992, pp. 3, 5).

[4] Myrdal and Myrdal (1934).

[5] Bok (1992, pp. 15–16).

[6] Myrdal and Myrdal (1934, p. 10).

[7] 'The word "crisis" in the book's title ... is no coincidence. More than just an attempt to inject drama, crisis is an integral component of all the texts produced by Alva and

In a 1935 pamphlet, Myrdal made a succinct statement of the reasons why an active population policy was needed.[8] At the time, he stated, fertility in Sweden had declined to a level that would lead to a future decline of the population. Myrdal did not believe that the concomitant increase of the capital-labor ratio would produce increased wages and reduced unemployment. The population decline would also lead to reduced production and the future, smaller, generations would have to support an increasing number of elderly, which in turn would lower their own living standard. That people opted for fewer children was not strange. There was a tradeoff between more children and an increased material standard, but this, in the long run, would be self-defeating.

Myrdal regarded the decline of the population as a cumulative process:

> … it is very doubtful whether a reduction of the population, once it has gathered momentum, can ever be broken at any population level. The issue *may* then not be that of a certain reduction of the population, which may perhaps not be so serious, but of an increasing, ever downward depopulation tendency, a movement towards the extinction of the population.[9]

Social Reform

In order to break the downward spiral, social reform measures were needed, and those should not just aim at a general increase of the standard of living of broad population segments, but at the reduction of the risks that threatened the subsistence and livelihood of the population and at securing employment and incomes for the families. It should contain measures that reduced the costs of having children. Incomes should be redistributed from people without children or with few children to families with more children as well as from richer to poorer people.

Gunnar Myrdal. Into the 1980s they still constantly invoke a situation of crisis or even despair'. Gunnar in particular repeatedly pointed to the importance of detecting dangers that stemmed from ignorance and opportunism. 'This … is typical of Gunnar's discourse from 1934 onward: a looming apocalypse but the opportunity to transform it into a hopeful future. The fact that not a single one of his predictions comes true does not prevent Gunnar from generating a constant litany of catastrophic scenarios' (Etzemüller 2014, pp. 115, 115–16).

[8] Myrdal (1935b).

[9] Ibid., pp. 10–11.

The growth of the Swedish population was out of equilibrium. The Myrdals, however, did not despair. On the contrary, as Thomas Etzemüller has noted, 'In none of their texts do Alva and Gunnar give up all hope. That would not fit with the constructive role of the social engineer. Instead … they evoke crisis to justify policies'.[10] The question, then, simply was what had to be done to stop the population decline.

The Myrdals did not share the conservative conviction, manifested in the prohibition of sales and information about contraceptives dating from 1910, that birth control was conducive to lax morals. They put the problem into a wider social context. The population problem was not unidimensional. The population could not be allowed to grow unless the economic and social conditions of the poor were improved. It was precisely here that they saw the *real* immorality—in the prevailing social order:

> A social order which, in spite of the fact that the rate of fertility has fallen far below the limit of reproduction and in spite of the trend being a downward one, does not afford to give the children sufficient and health food, and spacious dwellings that are not damp, safe health care and a good upbringing, and which *at the same time* has no use for large part of its labor force, which remains unemployed – this social order is senseless, irrational and immoral …[11]

This state of society, in turn, called for deep-going social engineering measures. Marginal adjustments would not do. Gunnar and Alva argued that the only way of simultaneously solving the problem of a potentially declining population and reducing the poverty they saw and documented was that of a combination of thorough reform of the Swedish society and a redistribution of incomes from the rich to the poor. Solving the poverty problem would create room for more people. Their project did not end there, however. It was part of a deep-going effort to change Swedish society. It was an effort to create a modernity hitherto unheard of in Sweden, what Yvonne Hirdman has called 'the hugest success ever of Swedish politics'[12]:

[10] Etzemüller (2014, p. 116).

[11] Myrdal and Myrdal (1934, p. 285).

[12] Hirdman (2006, p. 189).

> The population issue was the focus of the Myrdal's [sic] most celebrated attempt to use social engineering to rationalize and modernize Swedish society. Despite rapid urbanization and industrialization, many urban Swedes, in the Myrdals' view, suffered from a form of 'cultural lag' and continued to apply older, rural values to family life. What was needed was a new, planned socialist sense of community that was built on a broad, democratic foundation.[13]

The ambition of the Myrdals went far beyond the solution of the population problem. In the revised edition of their book, from 1935, they bluntly stated:

> For us the problem is: depopulation or social reform. And the program becomes: a new society permeated by social solidarity, where the entire nation to an increasing extent recognizes its shared responsibility for the children who will constitute the next generation. Only through the gradual realization of this society it will become possible to gradually destroy the narrow individualism that currently poisons every aspect of the life of our people and threatens its very existence.[14]

The most important reform issue was that of guaranteeing a satisfactory living standard for the families. Unless employment and subsistence risks could be substantially reduced and incomes increased, '*all other measures to increase marital fertility will be futile*'.[15] Families needed economic security if they were to have more children. In the first place, the entire labor force—including the women—had to be put to productive work. When the Myrdals were writing, women frequently had to stop working when they began to have children. Their presence was needed at home, but employers could also dismiss women who got married and/or bore children. The latter called for legislation and the former for new forms of childcare: collective forms, 'large nurseries', i.e., day-care centers. This amounted to a far-reaching program. As Thomas Etzemüller notes,

> Alva and Gunnar want nothing less than to raise an entirely new breed of people in order to overcome the 'excessive' and 'false' individualism

[13] Jackson (1990, p. 75). A detailed account of Alva and Gunnar Myrdal's project in the wider modernity context is provided by Etzemüller (2014).

[14] Myrdal and Myrdal (1935, pp. 16–17).

[15] Myrdal and Myrdal (1934, p. 187).

> that has generated so many 'atomized egotists.' These see children as the gateway. They must be liberated from discontented, overstressed parents and be brought up collectively in crèches and schools.[16]

But this was not enough. In order to guarantee the reproduction of the Swedish population, a 'rather radical redistribution of incomes between families with different child support burdens and different incomes' was required.[17] This social solidarity, in combination with a prophylactic population policy, that could serve to 'improve the quality of the human material', was necessary in order to ensure that the Swedish population once more would 'find it worthwhile to reproduce itself'.[18]

The Measures

The social recipe presented by the Myrdals involved a number of specific family policy measures. One was subsidized housing. It was not realistic to assume that families with several children could be crammed into one or two-room apartments.[19] The nutrition standard was another issue. Systematic statistics were lacking, but given the scant information available the Myrdals argued that 'Food scarcity is obviously still a pretty terrible reality for the majority of poor families with many children'.[20] That, together with the lack of balance in their diets, led to a rather pessimistic conclusion with respect to the nutrition standard in Sweden. This was partly an income problem, but also a question of popular education with respect to the composition of family expenditure.

[16] Etzemüller (2014, p. 112).

[17] Myrdal and Myrdal (1934, p. 11).

[18] Ibid.

[19] In 1933, together with the architect Uno Åhrén, one of the leading exponents of functionalism in Sweden, Gunnar, in a report from a governmental commission (SOU 1933:14) had commented on the dismal housing conditions prevailing among the working class. 'There is still … reason for the opinion that *the housing conditions of broad population segments are not such that from the social point of view they satisfy reasonable minimum requirements*' (ibid., p. 90). Far too many people lived in far too small low-standard apartments. The report made Minister of Social Affairs, Gustav Möller, appoint a government commission on social housing, which included both Myrdal and Åhrén, to formulate a new housing policy for Sweden.

[20] Myrdal and Myrdal (1934, p. 160).

Health care was another important issue. It was obvious to the Myrdals that the state had to assume the responsibility for both curative and—most importantly—prophylactic—care and that, in addition, it should be provided at zero cost to the citizens and not be dependent on the economic situation of the families. They also took issue with the educational system. The latter was utterly devoid of cultural sociological perspectives. The Swedish schools had to be reformed. They were disconnected from the current social development and did not prepare their pupils for 'complete participation in the new society'.[21] Alva and Gunnar were quite adamant about what they wanted the Swedish educational system to produce: 'If we ... first ask what kind of human type is promoted by the actual school system we find that the school work still aims at providing us with docile, non-reflecting, feudal beings and selfish private capitalists, that is human types adapted to an age long since past'.[22] In their view, asocial individualism and competition reigned supreme:

> This cultivation by the school of an exaggerated and false individualism, its suppression of the natural social attitude, to the extent that the school can really determine the future human type, is a dangerous result. You ought to play more carefully with the liberalistic idealization of the competitive ideal. [...]
>
> The school prolongs the mentality of the 1800s, the false individualism. Especially the socialists ought to keep this in mind. The socialist organization of production and the planned economy do not only imply a central, socially inclined and democratically decided direction of life in society but in addition and above all coordination. And the social psychological factor to build on is called education for cooperation.[23]

A new type of pedagogy, playing down traditional individual achievements and rewarding cooperation among the pupils and trial and error experimentation on part of the individual students was called for. The compulsory number of years in school—six—was far too low. It stopped short of the age when the children could begin to function along the lines sketched by the Myrdals. On the more practical level, Alva and Gunnar

[21] Ibid., p. 261.

[22] Ibid., p. 262.

[23] Ibid., p. 263.

presented a want list. They argued in favor of free school lunches for all children, free education, free textbooks, free transportation to school, free public pre-schools, kindergartens, after-school childcare, summer camps and grants for gifted children, large enough to cover their needs during the study years. They also stressed the necessity of freeing the subsidization from the stigma of poverty. In other words, the contributions were to be provided regardless of any proven need.[24]

A Hostile Reception

As could be expected, the population book by the Myrdals was not well received in all quarters. Its message was far too radical for that. Two of Gunnar's older colleagues reacted vary strongly: Gustav Cassel and Eli Heckscher, the latter together with his wife, Ebba. The criticism was presented in two of the most important Swedish daily newspapers.[25] In five articles in *Svenska Dagbladet*[26] Cassel contended that the approach rested on a socialist, or even communist, foundation and that the Myrdals had arranged their presentation of population question in such a way as to make a communist planned economy the only possible solution. What they were after was a radical restructuration of the Swedish society and their discussion of the population question simply served as a pretext for propagating this view. Cassel saw the costs of their program as prohibitive and took exception to the wholesale income and wealth redistribution advocated by them. Nevertheless, he conceded, the Myrdals were dealing with an important issue and agreed with them that social policy needed to be prophylactic and not just deal with symptoms.

The critique delivered by the Heckschers was far more acrimonious. The public part of it took place in four articles in *Dagens Nyheter*. In addition, they and the Myrdals exchanged fourteen lengthy, sharply formulated, private letters. The book had not proved the needs for such a radical program as they proposed and Gunnar and Alva did not understand the psychological causes of the birth decline but resorted to a monocausal, materialist, Marxist-inspired, explanation. Their motives were far from innocent. What the Myrdals wanted to do was to replace

[24] Ibid., p. 202.

[25] For a detailed account, see Carlson (1990, Chapter 4).

[26] The articles are included in Cassel (1935).

the traditional family with a collectivist upbringing, leaving the parents outside. In their private correspondence, the Heckschers called into question the moral of the Myrdals. Ebba even suggested that their program was totalitarian and that it came close to the social and family policies of the Nazis. The Myrdals took offense and in the end, Gunnar warned Eli Heckscher that the critique might destroy their future relationship. He accused him of resorting to cheap, moralistically shallow, dialectic and called him impossible to work with. Alva added that henceforth it would be difficult to remain on speaking terms with the Heckschers.

The Incipient Welfare State

The programmatic book by the Myrdals became the point of departure for 'virtually all the components of the welfare policy that were brought to the fore during the ... following decades'.[27] Gunnar was drafted to a number of government commissions on social issues between 1933 and 1938: on housing statistics, social housing, housing credit and agriculture. Most important, however, in 1935, after the debate that followed the book, the Swedish government appointed a commission to deal with the population issue, under the leadership of Nils Wohlin, professor of statistics and Member of Parliament. Myrdal joined the commission, which worked until 1938 and which produced almost one and a half dozen reports. Needless to say, with his restless energy, Myrdal became the primus motor of the commission, which allowed him to turn his ideas with respect to social engineering into practice and which laid the foundation for the modern Swedish population policy. He was the main or the only author of several of the reports published by the commission, e.g., on the sexual issue, abortion and nutrition, but he did not take any part in the drafting of the last reports, after a fallout with Wohlin.[28]

The population issue became the starting point for a large social reform program in Sweden, the realization of Prime Minister Per Albin Hansson's idea about the 'people's home' [*folkhemmet*], what internationally became known as 'the Swedish model'[29]:

[27] Gustafsson (1987–1989, p. 151).

[28] For a summary of the work of the commission and the subsequent political measures, see Carlson (1990, Chapters 5 and 6).

[29] Gustafsson (1998, p. 623).

> The population issue works like a catalyst. It lends every pressing sociopolitical problem the ghoulish glamor of the looming disaster, and a vast number of sociopolitical actors and institutions find a nodal point for their avid reformism. Sweden's political elite is relatively small and manageable, so the key actors are closely networked within institutions and enjoy a strong media presence. The investigative commissions systematize cooperation and evoke the impression of a holistic nexus. Every niche of social life is illuminated scientifically while all the sciences should gear themselves to the resolution of social problems: women's issues, child-rearing, nutrition, health, housing, kitchen equipment, and sexuality. Feminists, educators, doctors, architects, and nutritional scientists – no specialist need battle alone. This perpetuates a climate in which detailed charting ... of the entire nation appears normal, indeed vital, in order to rebuild the country through a common, positive effort. [...] No system is further [than the Swedish] from a totalitarian dictatorship. Yet virtually no system allows the state to undertake profound interventions into the integrity of individual human beings with so little fuss, should they reject utilitarianism to the detriment of the community.[30]

As William Barber puts it,

> The architecture of the Swedish welfare state was ... put in place under the smokescreen of the population argument. The radical measures taken were not justified on grounds that they were desirable per se. The rationale offered rested instead on the claim that they were essential to protecting the national interest from the hazards associate with population shrinkage.[31]

In a short magazine article from 1937, based on the principle report of the commission,[32] Myrdal stressed that the situation in Sweden was not one of islands of poverty in a landscape of generalized opulence. 'No', he wrote, 'the social problem still is, also in our case: *mass poverty*'.[33] However, hard statistical evidence, of the kind presented by

[30] Etzemüller (2014, pp. 119–20).

[31] Barber (2008, p. 59).

[32] SOU 1936:59, notably the appendix on the standard of living among Swedish families, written by the statistician Richard Sterner. Myrdal was the chairman of the group that produced the report and the main author of the latter.

[33] Myrdal (1937, p. 4).

the commission, was needed, for poverty had a tendency to go into hiding:

> The large apartments face the street; it is in the house across the yard that the masses live, in overpopulated small flats. When you travel in the country roads, the opulent large farms glitter, while the much more numerous ramshackle cottages hide away and even manage to look picturesque to those who do not live in them. The economically well off constitute a small share of the entire population, but they account for most of the debate. Most of them have no idea of the social reality.[34]

In order to improve the lot of the poor Myrdal advanced the same recipe as in the 1934 book: a combination of social policy and income transfers. He spoke of 'consumption socialism'. By seeing to it that the latter to a large extent took the form of public subsidies of housing, health care and education, it would be easier to improve the situation of the poor than by providing mere cash transfers. In the end, such a policy would also contribute to the production increases—the economic growth—that was necessary to come to grips with poverty in a sustainable way.

An Exaggerated Reputation?

Allan Carlson has argued that some later researchers have questioned the importance and originality of *Kris i befolkningsfrågan*. Writing in 1990, he stated that 'the deeper significance of the Myrdals' effort remains in dispute. For many decades, Swedish scholars regarded the Myrdals [sic] work on population as triggering "the breakthrough" of Modern Swedish social policy, the first full expression of and scientific justification for the complete welfare state'. However, according to Carlson[35]:

> Most recent interpreters of the Swedish population debate of the 1930s see the Myrdals primarily as popularizers of already extant policy ideas, in service to historically irresistible shifts in social organization. Historian Ann-Katrin Hatje,[36] for example, finds the Myrdals mere borrowers of existing political theories, with, if anything, too little appreciation for

[34] Ibid.

[35] Carlson (1990, p. 191).

[36] Hatje (1974).

> the changing roles of women and sexuality, which were driven by social and economic evolution. Ann-Sofie Kälvemark,[37] in her assessment of the effects of the pronatalist policies adopted in the 1930s, describes considerable confusion over goals, means, and results, suggesting that historical trends moved in spite of ideas and policy. In his provocative analysis of family decline in Sweden, sociologist David Poponoe[38] gives primary emphasis to socioeconomic currents that have produced what he calls 'the postnuclear family.' While cautious, he nonetheless shows the Myrdals' involvement as essentially an interesting ripple on a tidal wave of historical change.[39]

Carlson's interpretation of Hatje is unfair. Already in the first sentence of the first chapter of her book she states: 'The comprehensive and inventive Myrdal book, Kris i befolkningsfrågan, unfolded a number of problems of population policy whose causes in many cases were little known',[40] and in her introduction she writes: 'With the book by the Myrdal couple and the ensuing debate a new trend was begun in Swedish social policy …'[41]—opinions that hardly fit Carlson's description: 'Hatje … views their book and project as little more than a compilation of existing policy ideas, stitched together into a good – if less than original – public relations package'.[42]

Carlson's reading of Kälvemark is less biased. She accounts for prenatal efforts going on elsewhere in Europe—'In the 1920's pronatalist measures were … discussed and undertaken all over Europe'.[43] Kälvemark provides an account of this debate and the policies that were implemented elsewhere. However, in her own words, 'Compared to other European countries, Sweden at the beginning of the 1930's had very few policies designed positively to affect the fertility by alleviating the economic and/or other burdens of families. From this point of view the debate on population started almost at zero'.[44] In the early 1930s, especially

[37] Kälvemark (1980).

[38] Popenoe (1988).

[39] Carlson (1990, p. xii).

[40] Hatje (1974, p. 15).

[41] Ibid., p. 9.

[42] Carlson (1990, p. 191).

[43] Kälvemark (1980, p. 30).

[44] Ibid., p. 51.

the Conservative Party began to advocate pronatalist measures, but no practical measures came out of this. But then something happened:

> In 1934 ... a new phase in the debate was introduced when two prominent Social Democrats, Alva and Gunnar Myrdal, published a book entitled *Kris i befolkningsfrågan* (Crisis in the Population Question). Stressing the impending threat of population decline, the Myrdals demanded social reform as the only possible remedy for the situation. Neo-Malthusianism had played an important role in enabling the people to improve their living conditions by having fewer children, Now, however, society had to redistribute resources in order to give people the possibility of having the number of children they wanted – three per family was necessary to stop the threatening decline. [...] In their book the Myrdals also put forward a whole range of proposals for measures in the area, mainly directed at the economically least well situated parts of the population.[45]
>
> The Myrdals accounted for their position on the population question in an unusually extensive and coherent manner. Apart from their influence on the Swedish population policies of the 1930's ... they also have a special significance in having more than anyone else propagated their views on Swedish population policy, its main goals and most important expressions to a domestic and international audience.[46]

The influence of the Myrdals on the debate and policy formulation in Sweden is thus obvious in Kälvemark's book as well. The main thrust is, however, in a different direction. She demonstrates that all Swedish policies related to population policies did not have the intended effects. Her conclusion is clear-cut: 'Although for years the Swedish population policies of the 1930's have been considered successful, the results of this study indicate that the pronatalist goals were, at best, only partially realised'.[47]

The case of David Popenoe, finally, is simple. Nowhere in the chapter that deals with the role of the Myrdals does he put them into the fold of those who advocated a 'postnuclear' family. On the contrary, as Popenoe states himself:

> Despite their strong leftist political leanings, the Myrdals actually had a relatively conservative view of the family, its role in society, and its path

[45] Ibid., pp. 52, 53.

[46] Ibid., p. 55.

[47] Ibid., p. 138.

> of change. They saw the family as perhaps the main social institution in society, and they oriented the thrust of their policies toward what they regarded as the family's principal function: the socialization of children. Mainly because of its child-rearing functions, the family was something to be protected and enhanced. This put the Myrdals in an ideological camp quite apart from the antifamily tendencies of many radicals in Scandinavia, those who favored a radical change in the structure, if not the outright abolition, of the family.[48]

And, states Popenoe: 'It was the Myrdals' family ideology that was to prevail in Sweden over the next few decades. New family ideologies were to come, but they too were anticipated by the Myrdals …'[49]

Be that as it may. Carlson views the importance of *Kris i befolknings-frågan* and the later work of the Myrdals in a different, more long-term, light:

> … close analysis of the Myrdals as historical actors reveals a different picture: In a fundamental way, their application of intellectual muscle and political and intellectual skills altered the course of their society. Not the social trends they decried, nor the policies they sought, nor the results they achieved were immutable workings of history. Rather, they used the power of ideas to redirect Sweden in radically new ways. In pursuit of social revolution they foreclosed other options and possibilities and so served as progenitors of the postfamily welfare state.[50]

Carlson is not alone in his opinion. As we have already seen, Yvonne Hirdman presented the social engineering project of the Myrdals as the number one success story of Swedish politics, and, writing twenty-four years later, in 2014, Thomas Etzemüller concluded: 'Their book effectively condenses the sociopolitical approaches and problems of the previous decades and symbolizes the vital social reforms that Alva and Gunnar seek to implement'.[51] What is more,

> … the intense media debate over the Myrdals' book makes an impression on the political parties, and a feature film even takes up the same

[48] Popenoe (1988, p. 115).

[49] Ibid., p. 117.

[50] Carlson (1990, p. xii).

[51] Etzemüller (2014, p. 116).

> theme. Within just six months, in the spring of 1935, the political sphere is showing its willingness to improve the lot of women, children, and families, through sociopolitical reforms. In May Social Minister Gustav Möller appoints the first Population Commission.[52]

As we know, the commission was dominated by Gunnar Myrdal. What this boils down to is the fact that it is impossible to contend that the development of social policy that took place in Sweden in the 1930s would have unfolded without the Myrdals. They may have been the children of their time—who isn't?—and may have borrowed ideas that were floating around by then—no man is an island—but to argue that they did not steep them in their own mold and that Swedish social history would have been largely the same is simply not possible. They had an impact and it is impossible to think them out of the context which they contributed so actively to change.

The Godkin Lectures

Gunnar Myrdal returned to the population issue in his 1938 Godkin Lectures at Harvard, published as a book two years later,[53] using Sweden as the main illustration. He noted that poorer families in general had the largest number of children[54] and that in 'western civilization' a higher average standard of living could be achieved with a stationary population rather than with a declining one.[55] Myrdal considered it impossible to attain an increasing trend. Taking into account that all families would not be of the same size, keeping the Swedish population constant, he argued, meant that 'the fulfillment of this norm for population policy is incompatible not merely with the "two-child system" advocated by Neo-Malthusianism, but also with a "three-child system". In fact, our population goal almost implies that the ordinary, non-sterile marriage should aim at four children'.[56]

[52] Ibid., p. 117.

[53] Myrdal (1962a).

[54] Ibid., pp. 48–49, 172.

[55] Ibid., p. 130. He had drawn the same conclusions in the appendix that he, together with the statistician Sven Wicksell, contributed to the principle report of the Population Commission (SOU 1936:59, pp. 292, 295).

[56] Myrdal (1962a, p. 176).

Poorer families as a rule had more children than richer ones, but Myrdal thought it unreasonable that the responsibility for avoiding the decline of the Swedish population should be placed on the poor:

> In a democratic society we cannot accept a way of things whereby the poor, ignorant, and inexperienced maintain the stock of population. In a democratic society we must definitely direct our attention to the abolition of both poverty and ignorance, that is to say the very factors which for a long time have stimulated a high birth rate; we must do so even though the abundance of children produced by these factors is the only thing at present which prevents the population from being even more catastrophic than it is.[57]

An Institutional Approach

Myrdal's involvement with practical social policy made him focus on the institutions of society. In his 1935 inaugural lecture, he hinted that economic analysis needed a holistic approach:

> In a coherent economic policy, there exist no longer any special problems; all special problems are interconnected. The consequence of this for economic research and education is that specialist knowledge is of little value. [...] The study of economics hence to an increasing extent will be a study of the entire economy.[58]

Myrdal had by then begun to build up his latter-day conviction that in the study of society you have to take into account that all the variables that constitute it interact in a circular (and cumulative) fashion.[59] Later in his

[57] Ibid., p. 189.

[58] Myrdal (1935a, pp. 37–38).

[59] Carlson (2013) provides a chronological account of the findings of a number of stories of Myrdal's conversion to institutionalism. Possibly, Myrdal hade been playing with the idea for a long time. As early as 1919, in a newspaper article, dealing with the lack of ideas of his contemporary students, Myrdal complained about the exaggerated concentration on the own discipline (cited by Andersson 1989, p. 44):

> It used to be the privilege of the students to present wide, universal and idealistic views of everyday events. Now – during the great ... world war, during political upheaval and revolutions of geological dimensions, now, when a new era is dawning in the world and our country, with new tasks and new topics with respect to the

life, he would frequently refer to his early years as an economist as a period characterized by 'central theory'. As a young man, he looked down on the American institutionalists like Thorstein Veblen, John R. Commons and Wesley C. Mitchell. The latter two were still alive and Myrdal met them. He spent a month with Commons in Madison, Wisconsin, in 1930, but the only compliment he offered was: 'I remember he taught me bowling'. Looking back at his visit thirty-eight years later he stressed that at the time he 'was not converted to what was then called "the new economics,"'[60] a conviction that was strengthened during the early 1930s:

> ... the courageous trend in the late Twenties toward an institutional approach had a brief existence in the United States. What I believe nipped it in the bud was the world-wide economic depression. Faced by this great calamity, we economists of the 'theoretical' school, accustomed to reason in terms of simplified macro-models, felt we were on top of the situation, while the institutionalists were left in the muddle. It was at this stage that economists in the stream of the Keynesian revolution adjusted their theoretical models to the needs of the time, which thus gave victory much more broadly to our 'theoretical' approach.[61]
>
> When the further rise of institutional economics, which I then saw as a danger was averted, I believe this was an effect of the Great Depression. In the macroeconomic neoclassical school there were those of us who could master the problem of decreasing demand and deflation and give

> problems of society and life, the student appears to completely lack the ability to widen his views and opinions beyond the narrow circle of himself and his own special discipline.

Also, Gilles Dostaler (1990, p. 216) maintains that 'the oft-mentioned, so-called, clear-cut dividing line in Myrdal's intellectual development does not exist'. The basis for this contention is that already during the early years of his career, 1927–1934, notably in *The Political Element in the Development of Economic Theory*, he employed some of the concepts and ideas that would characterized what is commonly thought of as the 'institutionalist' phase of his life. '... one must be suspicious of any allegations of a change in outlook, a break, or a radical transformation in Myrdal's work. It is too complex to be cut up into mere parts' (ibid., p. 199). The argument in the present book amounts to much the same: Myrdal gradually—over forty years—built the methodology that would be brought to full fruition in *Asian Drama*.

[60] Myrdal (1978a, p. 771).

[61] Myrdal (1974, p. 7).

relevant policy advice to governments, while the institutionalists remained disoriented.[62]

From High Theory to Institutionalism

In just a few years, Gunnar Myrdal was to change his methodological approach.[63] The population book was as much sociological as it was economic, arguably even more, and being involved in a number of government commissions in the 1930s forced him to concentrate on practical social issues which most of the time were multidimensional and called for solutions based on several social sciences. He has himself described his change of course:

> Meanwhile, I had become an institutional economist. In Sweden I became involved in social equality problems, which I found could not be handled scientifically except by broadening the approach to all human relations. In 1938 I accepted responsibility for a study of race relations in the United States, and this took me farther away from conventional economics. I found myself writing a book about the entire American civilization, with stress on various aspects relevant from the viewpoint of the largest of the disadvantaged groups here.
>
> From then on more definitely I came to see that there are no economic, sociological, or psychological problems, but just problems, and they are all mixed and composite. In research, the only permissible demarcation is between relevant and irrelevant conditions. The problems are regularly also political and, moreover, must be seen in historical perspective.[64]

As Richard Swedberg has pointed out, 'Exactly when Myrdal became an institutionalist is not clear'.[65] What matters is *that* he became one, sometime during the 1930s. As Benny Carlson puts it: 'Myrdal eventually became – alongside John Kenneth Galbraith – the world's most renowned institutional economist',[66] and Kurt Dopfer goes even further:

[62] Myrdal (1978a, p. 772).

[63] Van Loo (1989) stresses the unique in Myrdal's institutional approach and his later application of it to the problem of economic development. She deals with it as a shift of paradigm in the sense of Thomas Kuhn (1970).

[64] Myrdal (1978a, p. 772). Cf. Myrdal (1969, pp. 10–11).

[65] Swedberg (1990, p. xii).

[66] Carlson (2013, p. 512).

'His reputation as an institutional economist grew to such an extent in later years that most are unaware today that he started his scientific career as a traditional monetary economist'.[67] James Angresano, who has traced Myrdal's development from an economist concentrating on 'high theory' to an institutional interdisciplinary social scientist,[68] offers the following characteristic of his approach:

> Myrdal's perspective towards an economy was evolutionary-institutional. He viewed the economy not as a static entity, but as an ongoing process comprised of the aggregate of institutions which perform economic functions and determine economic conditions. These institutions behave according to working rules, many of which are established by authorities who allocate scarce resources while answering questions pertaining to production and distribution of goods and services. Working rules establish rights and duties of the economy's participants, and serve to create order among conflicting interests while strengthening the social process for coordinating economic (as well as social, political, and cultural) matters by outlining the boundaries of behavior for economic activity. Societies establish institutions and working rules in an attempt to achieve order – predictability without rigidity and flexibility without chaos.[69]

The working rules are of two kinds, formal and informal, and they operate at many levels of society, from the micro subjects to the whole nation. The formal rules establish the rights and duties of both the individuals and the state and they establish the property rights system within which the economic transactions take place. The informal rules (attitudes and opinions) in turn provide a basis for the establishment of formal rules by expressing the views of the citizens on the conditions that ought to prevail in society and on the existing conditions.

[67] Dopfer (1988, p. 227).

[68] Angresano (1981, 1997).

[69] Angresano (1997, pp. 1–2).

CHAPTER 4

An American Dilemma

The book about American civilization that Myrdal referred to was of course *An American Dilemma*.[1] In the summer of 1937, he had received an invitation from Frederick Keppel, the president of the Carnegie Corporation in New York, to lead an investigation of the 'Negro problem' in the United States—the position of blacks in American society and the relations between whites and blacks. Keppel wanted a researcher from 'a country with no background or traditions of imperialism' in order to make the investigation acceptable to blacks.[2] As he pointed out in his foreword to *An American Dilemma*, that only left Switzerland and Sweden, and in the end, the offer went to Myrdal,[3] who accepted and, in September 1938, left Sweden for the United States together with his family and the statistician Richard Sterner, who would become one of the members of his team. Myrdal and Sterner began their work with a two-month tour through the American South, where at the time the vast majority of blacks were disenfranchised, meeting all kinds of people, to

[1] Myrdal (1944a).

[2] Jackson (1990, p. xiii).

[3] Keppel (1944, p. vi).

M. Lundahl, *The Dynamics of Poverty*, Palgrave Studies in the History of Economic Thought,
https://doi.org/10.1007/978-3-030-73347-6_4

get firsthand on-the-ground experience before they began reading the relevant literature.[4]

In the preface to the study, Myrdal spells out the all-embracing terms of reference:

> The study … should aim at determining the social, political, educational, and economic status of the Negro in the United States as well as defining opinions held by different groups of Negroes and whites as to his 'right' status. It must, further, be concerned with both recent changes and current trends with respect to the Negro's position in American society. Attention must also be given to the total American picture with particular emphasis on relations between the two races. Finally, it must consider what changes are being or can be induced by education, legislation, interracial efforts, concerted action by Negro groups, etc.[5]

Gunnar Myrdal put together a team of six researchers plus thirty-one independent scholars for work on different themes. The team included Ralph Bunche, at the time professor of political science at the black Howard University in Washington DC. His later career unfolded within the United Nations. Bunche managed to negotiate the armistice between Israel and the Arab countries in 1949, for which he was awarded the Nobel Peace Prize the following year. Myrdal toured the South with him in 1939. Another team member was Arnold Rose, a mere twenty-three-year-old sociologist from the University of Chicago, who with time would become professor at the University of Minnesota.

The team members produced draft manuscripts,[6] but in the end, Myrdal wrote the entire text with Sterner and Rose, who figure as co-authors of the book. His work was interrupted by the German invasion of Norway and Denmark on April 9, 1940. Myrdal naturally feared that Sweden was next and decided to go home and offer his services to his country. He was back in March 1941, spending the first four weeks in Jackson, Mississippi, where he read the manuscripts that had been finished

[4] Myrdal's own account of the work with the book is found in Myrdal (1987), a book dictated during the last years of his life. For a brilliant scholarly account of the history of *An American Dilemma*, see Jackson (1990).

[5] Myrdal (1944a, pp. x–xi).

[6] Several were published as books, most notably the one by the social anthropologist Melville Herskovits (1941).

by his team members, but not only that: 'In Jackson … I found out how the Jim Crow system worked in the deepest South'.[7]

In August 1942, the manuscript was finished: a monumental study of almost 1,500 pages.[8] Given the limits of the present essay, it is impossible to go into any details of this incredibly impressive book—arguably the best Myrdal ever wrote. William Barber pinpoints the 'encyclopedic dimensions' of it.[9]

What matters in the present context is how Myrdal viewed the 'Negro problem', how he analyzed it and how he purported to solve it. His views rested on explicit value premises, institutionalism, circular, cumulative causation and social engineering.

The 'Negro Problem'

At the time when Myrdal began his study, the 'Negro problem' was viewed mainly as an economic problem. In one sense, it was true. Poverty among blacks was of one of the main ingredients of the racial issue. 'The Great Depression created unprecedented levels of deprivation among Afro-Americans in the cities of the North and the South and triggered a crisis in southern agriculture with far-reaching consequences for American race relations', summarizes Walter Jackson.[10] In 1932, the worst year of the depression, black unemployment in the major cities could run as high as 50 percent and in 1935, one-third of the black population was on relief. In the South, low agricultural prices made poor black tenant farmers face the unpalatable choice of either leaving agriculture or trying to survive on drastically reduced incomes.[11]

Myrdal himself offers a succinct summary evaluation of the appalling living conditions of the American blacks:

> The economic situation of the Negroes in America is pathological. Except for a small minority enjoying upper or middle class status, the masses of American Negroes, in the rural South and in the segregated slum quarters

[7] Myrdal (1987, p. 29).

[8] Myrdal (1944a).

[9] Barber (2008, p. 74).

[10] Jackson (1990, p. 1).

[11] Ibid., pp. 2–3.

> in Southern and Northern cities, are destitute. They own little property; even their household goods are mostly inadequate and dilapidated. Their incomes are not only low but irregular. They thus live from day to day and have scant security for the future. Their entire culture and their individual interests and strivings are narrow.[12]

The blacks were concentrated in the poorest part of the country, the South, in agriculture, which was a depressed industry, notably cotton cultivation. They seldom owned land but were sharecroppers or wage laborers. Few worked outside the agricultural sector, and if they did, it was in low-paid services or in unskilled jobs in manufacturing. Unemployment rates were much higher, proportionally, among blacks than among whites. At the same time, in the South, blacks were held to be inferior to whites. Myrdal asked why this was so. He described them not as a class or a race, but as a 'caste'. In the South, even the richest blacks were considered inferior to the poorest whites. 'Caste' was a very strong term, but the circumstances were such that Myrdal considered it warranted:

> Myrdal's use of caste developed from his conception of Negro status as being determined by whites. If whites refused to intermarry with blacks, if they confronted blacks with insuperable social barriers that did not exist for white immigrant groups, then, Myrdal reasoned, the term *caste* was justified. Myrdal deployed the word *caste* to highlight the contradiction between the American ideology of open competition and the practice of excluding Afro-Americans from rising freely in the white class system.[13]

According to the conventional American wisdom of the time, racial prejudice would disappear as economic and social standards improved among whites and blacks. Outside the South, it was seen as a southern problem, and in the South, it was not considered a problem at all. Myrdal, however, did not accept this—what he thought of as simplistic—explanation. He reintroduced the moral element into the discussion—on the very first line of his introduction to the book. The United States was an eminently moralistic society, he argued. A liberal set of values, rooted in the Enlightenment, in Christianity and in English law, an *ethos*, of which all Americans were conscious, existed. These principles, which ought to

[12] Myrdal (1944a, p. 205).

[13] Jackson (1990, p. 220).

rule, Myrdal called the 'American Creed'. They constituted the foundation of American nationalism and they encompassed democracy, equality, freedom, fair opportunity and the rule of law.

However, it was precisely here that Myrdal saw the 'American Dilemma'. The American Creed built on 'high national and Christian precepts', but 'the valuations on specific planes of individual and group living' often diverged substantially from the former.[14] This created a conflict within the individual, which in turn affected his behavior, and made him pay lip service to the ideals in a number of concrete situations. The 'Negro problem' was an outstanding case in point: 'a moral issue of conflicting valuations'.[15] Myrdal argued that it was necessary 'to give *primary* attention to what goes on in the minds of white Americans'.[16] As his collaborator Richard Sterner expressed it more than twenty-five years later, 'The very approach to the subject that Myrdal employed was prone to make people sit up and think'.[17] Virtually all power in the United States was held by the whites, who hence determined the 'place' of the blacks in American society:[18] 'precarious, uncertain and changing'.[19] Myrdal did not stop there, however:

> In addition to making his argument about the conflict in the minds of white Americans, Myrdal presented a structural argument that a conflict between the American creed and racial discrimination existed within American institutions. He presented the case against scientific theories of inherited differences in intelligence and temperament among the races; he marshaled an enormous array of evidence to show discrimination in the economy, political system, and courts; he sketched a disturbing picture of the damage that segregation and racial discrimination inflicted on blacks; and he analyzed competing strategies within the black protest movement.[20]

[14] Myrdal (1944a, p. xlvii).

[15] Ibid., p. l.

[16] Ibid., p. li.

[17] Sterner (1971, p. 56).

[18] Myrdal (1944a, p. li).

[19] Ibid., p. liii.

[20] Jackson (1990, p. 186).

Explicit Value Premises

Gunnar Myrdal spent two appendices in *An American Dilemma* on the problem of values and value premises.[21] He was eminently aware of the fact that 'Negro problem' was a hot potato which could easily invite criticism against the researcher for being partial. But not only that. Ever since his investigation of the dubious objectivity of his fellow economists in their intervention in the public debate and economic policy issues, he had been convinced, as a matter of principle, that economics was not a value-free discipline. In *An American Dilemma*, he extended his perspective to encompass all the other social sciences. 'The younger social sciences', he wrote, 'have followed much the same track'.[22]

The extension was logical, since, as we will soon see, there he also excluded the use of just economics to analyze the racial issue, and he did not attempt to uphold any line of distinction between the positive and normative aspects of economics. Valuations creep into all aspects of the social sciences. The social scientist lives in a culture full of preconceptions and biases of all kinds, some of which he is likely to share, consciously or unconsciously. Hence, in order to avoid biased results, the best that the researcher can do is to make his value premises explicit. Furthermore, any old value premises won't do. The premises must be chosen according to certain rules and they must be relevant for the society under study.

The problem of value premises, Myrdal argued, is present from the very beginning of scientific investigation. 'The full statement of a problem, including the decision of scope, direction, hypothesis, classification principles, and the definition of all terms used, renders explicit the valuations necessary in fact-finding research … If … practical usefulness is an aim in science, even the direction of research becomes dependent upon much wider valuations considering society'.[23] In other words, all research decisions are based on value premises, and the best you can do is to make them explicit.

The danger of biased results was exceptionally high in the case of the 'Negro problem':

[21] Myrdal (1944a, Appendix 1 and 2).

[22] Ibid., p. 1048.

[23] Ibid., p. 1058.

> Race problems, generally, and the Negro problem in America, particularly, are to an extraordinary degree affected by conflicting valuations of high emotional tension. Keeping in mind the actual power situation in the American nation and observing the prevalent opinions in the dominant white group, we are led, even by a superficial examination, to expect that even the scientific biases will run against the Negroes most of the time.[24]

Myrdal identified six possible classes of scientific biases in the case of the American race problem: the scale of 'friendliness' to blacks, the scale of 'friendliness' to the South, the scale of radicalism-conservatism (*'In a sense this is the master scale of biases in the social sciences'*), the scale of optimism-pessimism, the scale of integration-isolation (the tendency to treat the race problem in isolation from the total complex of problems in American society) and, finally, the scale of scientific integrity (the degree to which the scientist is prepared to state 'plainly and clearly' unpopular conclusions).[25] The value premises that Myrdal himself chose for *An American Dilemma* were precisely what he called the American Creed.

Circular, Cumulative Causation

The terms of reference pointed directly to the need for an analytical method that cut across all the social sciences, and Myrdal had it. In *An American Dilemma*, he applied the approach that he had originally encountered in Wicksell's monetary writings: that of circular, cumulative causation. Although he had played with the idea before, as we have seen, it was in this book that he wholeheartedly embraced for the first time the idea of a total view of an economic and social problem in terms of a circular and cumulative process—rejecting the notion of stable equilibrium—where all the constituent parts interacted with each other. In this process, no single part was more important than the other.[26] Economic, social, cultural and moral factors all had to be brought into the picture to explain the situation. It was their interaction that made for the outcome. Myrdal identified three groups of factors which all reinforced each other in a cumulative fashion so as to keep the blacks at the bottom of American society but which could also interact in the opposite direction:

[24] Ibid., p. 1035.

[25] Ibid., p. 1040.

[26] The notion permeates the entire book. See, however, especially ibid., Appendix 3.

> The scheme of causal interrelation is as important in explaining why Negroes are so poor and in evaluating the wider social effects of Negro poverty. The dynamics of the problem is this: A primary change, induced or unplanned, affecting any one of the three bundles of interdependent causative factors – (1) the economic level; (2) standards of intelligence, ambition, health, education, decency, manners, and morals; and (3) discrimination by whites – will bring changes in the other two and, through mutual interaction, move the whole system along in one direction or another. No single factor, therefore, is the 'final cause' in a theoretical sense.[27]

In a retrospective on his methodology in 1978, Myrdal spelled out his institutional circular causation approach:

> The most fundamental thought that holds institutional economists together is our recognition that even if we focus attention on specific problems, our study must take into account the entire social system, including everything else of importance for what comes to happen in the economic field. Foremost, among other things, is the distribution of power in society and, more generally, economic, social, and political stratification; indeed, all institutions and attitudes. To this must be added, as an exogenous set of factors, induced policy measures, applied with the purpose of changing one or several of these endogenous factors.
>
> The dynamics of this social system are determined by the fact that among all the endogenous conditions there is *circular causation*, implying that, if there is change in one condition, others will change in response. Those secondary changes in their turn will cause new changes all around, even affecting the conditions whose change we assumed initiated the process, and so on in further rounds. So the whole system will be moving in one direction or another, and it may even be turning around its axis. There is no one basic factor; everything causes everything else. This implies *interdependence* within the whole social process. And there is generally no equilibrium in sight.[28]

Summing up, stated Myrdal: 'These remarks are offered as hints toward the master model of institutional economics. That model must be holistic, even when focused on particular economic problems'.[29]

[27] Ibid., p. 208.

[28] Myrdal (1978a, pp. 773–74).

[29] Ibid., p. 775.

An American Dilemma constituted an important methodological step for Myrdal.[30] Applied to the 'Negro problem':

> Throughout this inquiry, we shall assume a general interdependence between all factors in the Negro problem. White prejudice and discrimination keep the Negro low in standards of living, health, education, manners and morals. This, in its turn, gives support to white prejudice. White prejudice and Negro standards thus mutually 'cause' each other. If things remain about as they are and have been, this means that the two forces happen to balance each other. Such a static 'accommodation' is, however, entirely accidental. If either of the factors changes, this will cause a change in the other factor, too, and start a process of interaction where the change in one factor will continuously be supported by the reaction of the other factor. The whole system will be moving in the direction of the primary change, but much further. This is what we mean by cumulative causation.[31]

Myrdal clarifies:

> If now, in this hypothetically balanced state, for some reason or other, the Negro plane of living should be lowered, this will – other things being equal – in its turn increase white prejudice. Such an increase in white prejudice has the effect of pressing down further still the Negro plane of living, which again will increase prejudice, and so on, by way of mutual interaction between the two variables, ad infinitum. A cumulative process is thus set in motion which can have final effects quite out of proportion to the magnitude of the original push.[32]

[30] Gunnar Myrdal used the notion in other contexts as well. In 1941, he and Alva reported home in a book about the American society (Myrdal and Myrdal 1941). The idea behind the book was to present a society which most Swedes were ignorant about, and they did a good job. The book also reveals an interest in poverty and social issues, manifested above all in a lengthy account of American social policy and its change over time. This is not the place to go into any details, but let us notice a single sentence in the book: 'Social contexts are always cumulative' (ibid., p. 93). Later, this idea is applied to the problem of why the labor union movement was so weak in the US. Myrdal's answer is that it was weak because it is weak, in a circular fashion. The union movement was weak because the political labor movement was weak and vice versa (ibid., pp. 227–28).

[31] Myrdal (1944a, pp. 75–76).

[32] Ibid., p. 1066.

This principle operates also when the principal components are split into sub-components, so an increase in one of the constituent parts of the black standard of living would tend to increase the others as well:

> A rise in Negro employment, for instance, will raise family incomes, standards of nutrition, housing, and health the possibilities of giving the Negro youth more education, and so forth, and all these effects of the initial change, will, in their turn, improve the Negroes' possibilities of getting employment and earning a living. The original push could have been some other factor than employment, say, for example, an improvement of health or educational facilities for Negroes. Through action and interaction the whole system of the Negro's 'status' would have been set in motion in the direction indicated by the first push.[33]

It does not matter where you start. The entire system will move in the same direction as the original change and furthermore feeds back on the latter.[34]

An American Dilemma is divided into eleven very detailed 'parts', each one with a number of variables which interact with each other. In

[33] Ibid., p. 76.

[34] As Trevor Swan (1962) later demonstrated, the process is not necessarily cumulative (unstable). It may as well converge to a stable equilibrium. For the cumulative process to arise, white prejudices must be sufficiently sensitive to change in black living standards and vice versa. The situation may be depicted in a diagram with black standards on the y-axis and white prejudices on the x-axis. Swan draws two linear reaction curves: aa (the reaction of black standards to a change in white prejudices) and bb (the reaction of white prejudices to a change in black standards) and shows that for the unstable situation to arise the bb line must cut the aa curve from below. This describes the situation where a single equilibrium exists. Swan, however, considers that situation unrealistic (ibid., pp 424–25):

> The unstable equilibrium case – *bb* cutting *aa* from below – seems *too* unstable to serve even as a 'simplified' mental model' for many purposes. The slightest breeze can puff Uncle Tom's cabin either into the heaven of White brotherhood or into the limbo of extinction. The stable case – *bb* cutting *aa* from above – seems *too* stable. Only a permanent shift in the structure of social forces can change the equilibrium point. Is there no counterpart in the model for our instinctive feeling that an initial 'explosion' of some kind – a war or depression, a rape or a lynching – may disrupt a pre-existing stable equilibrium and lead to an entirely new social situation?

Swan suggests that there may be limiting factors that work to stop cumulation (ibid., p. 425):

the first, Myrdal presents his approach and introduces his value premises. The second deals with various facets of 'race' and the third with the black population and its migration. The long fourth part scrutinizes the place of blacks in the American economy with particular emphasis on discrimination. Next, the race issue is analyzed as a political problem and in the sixth part Myrdal deals with the functioning of the American justice system. Two parts analyze social inequality and social stratification and another two deal with various aspects of black leadership and the black community. The last part of the book is forward-looking. It explores the trends in race relations and black economic and social status in the light of the wartime experience.

An American Dilemma was no conventional study:

> What … made his exposition unique was that he, much more consequently than others, broke with the tendency to regard the racial issue as a segregated isolate in American social life. What he studied was *the entire USA*

> When the Negroes (on the average) approach the standards of the Whites, some of the latter grow jealous and any further improvement in Negro standards causes little reduction of White prejudice, and may even cause it to increase; on the other hand, when the Negroes are very poor the White stomach for prejudice is satiated and perhaps compassion is aroused.

If similar limiting factors are present in the black community as well, the aa curve, looked at from the y-axis, may be S-shaped and the bb curve looked at from the x-axis may have the shape of an inverted S. Then the two curves twist around each other and produce a situation with three equilibrium points. In the high one, white prejudices are weak and black standards high. In the low one, white prejudices are strong and black standards are low. These two points are stable equilibria. Any departures from them will generate reactions that bring the system back to the original equilibrium. The intermediate point, with mid-level white prejudices and black standards, on the other hand, is unstable. Any departure from it will send the system either to the high-level or low-level equilibrium.

This, in turn, has consequences for the possibility of using social engineering. Using the undesirable low-level equilibrium, as the starting point, the first one consists in finding measures that lift the aa curve until the unstable equilibrium point is converted into a point of tangency between the two curves. In that case, the system becomes stable downwards, but unstable upwards, which allows for measures that lead to a cumulative upward movement until the desired high-level equilibrium point is reached. The second case assumes that the curves are unchanged. This requires a push which is big enough to move the system all the way from the unstable equilibrium to the stable high-level point. According to Swan, the multiple equilibrium situation constitutes a much better description of the real world than Myrdal's original suggestion in *An American Dilemma*.

viewed from its backyard – the development of its politics, economy, agriculture, education, social care, social life, church matters, organizations, etc.[35]

Social Engineering

In *An American Dilemma*, Myrdal took issue with the conventional American wisdom by arguing that the 'Negro problem' was essentially a 'white man's problem', caused by racial discrimination. When it came to racial relations, White America did not adhere to the American Creed, especially not to the equality part of it. People had no problems justifying or rationalizing their prejudices. Many of the attitudes of the whites were rooted in ignorance and lack of concern. Myrdal hence concluded that '*the social engineering required should have its basis in a deliberate and well-planned campaign of popular education*'.[36]

Myrdal made it clear from the beginning that he was concentrating on the *solution* of the 'Negro problem'. His study would be concerned with social engineering.[37] This conviction grew stronger during the course of the work, notably after his visits to the South. As Walter Jackson observes, 'After Myrdal saw the desperate poverty of most Afro-Americans, the system of legalized segregation and discrimination, and the racial violence in the South, the research project became a challenge of the utmost personal importance to him'.[38]

The existence of circular, cumulative causation, Myrdal noted, had a practical corollary. It opened for the possibility of effecting an upward push on the overall situation of blacks through any of the variables in the system, although in practice no rational policy would work by changing a single factor: 'the rational refutation of so-called panaceas'.[39] By the same token, it was bound to encourage the reformer.

[35] Sterner (1971, pp. 58–59).

[36] Myrdal (1944a, p. 383).

[37] Jackson (1990, pp. 89, 106).

[38] Ibid., p. 132.

[39] Ibid., p. 77.

In an article published in the Swedish *Vi* magazine in 1943 (later reprinted in a book of essays),[40] written after he had finished *An American Dilemma*, Myrdal summarized the recent development of the racial issue in the United States under the pressure of the on-going war. Racial prejudice was still strong in the South, while at the same time, blacks were becoming more and more aware of their legal rights. Research had convincingly demonstrated that no intrinsic differences existed in the mental faculties of the races. The former white ideology on this point lay in ruins. In their war effort, the Americans had to preach the gospel of equality between the races, which in turn called for an application of the same principles back home. There, however, the picture was split. The American legislation supported the blacks, and so did, to an increasing extent, the northern whites; but in the South the endeavors to subdue blacks continued, outside the law.

Still, Myrdal was optimistic. The war effort constituted a positive influence. The United States had to defend the idea of equality between the races in the face of Hitler's attempt to exterminate the Jews, and this, in turn, made it more difficult to maintain racial discrimination at home. Myrdal thought that he saw a change coming and invoked the American Creed, which in the end he hoped would overcome racial prejudice. In the preface to *An American Dilemma* he wrote:

> When looking back over the long manuscript, one main conclusion – which should be stressed here since it cannot be reiterated through the whole book – is this: that *not since Reconstruction has there been more reason to anticipate fundamental changes in American race relationships, changes which will involve a development toward the American ideals.*[41]

At the end of the book, Myrdal came back to the opportunity of the United States to turn the vicious circle that characterized the racial situation into a virtuous one. 'What America is constantly reaching for is democracy at home and abroad. The main trend in its history is the gradual realization of the American Creed. [...] America can demonstrate that justice, equality and cooperation is possible between white and colored people'.[42] Myrdal was optimistic, but not unqualifiedly so. The

[40] Myrdal (1943a, b), respectively.

[41] Myrdal (1944a, p. xix).

[42] Ibid., p. 1021.

situation required a conscious choice: '*America is free to choose whether the Negro shall remain her liability or become her opportunity*'.[43]

The Importance of *An American Dilemma*

Walter Jackson calls *An American Dilemma* 'one of the most influential works of social science ever written in America'.[44] It sold more than 100,000 copies. William Barber refers to it as 'one of the few works of scholarship to alter the course of history'[45] and Thomas Sowell offers the following appreciation of it: 'If there was a single book that might be said to mark the turning point in thinking about race among the intelligentia, it would be ***An American Dilemma*** by Swedish economist Gunnar Myrdal, published in 1944'.[46] Sowell continues:

> Gunnar Myrdal's basic premise – that racial problems in America were fundamentally problems inside the heads of white people, and that the resulting discrimination or neglect explained black-white differences in economic and other outcomes – was to remain the fundamental assumption of liberal thinking and policies for decades thereafter.[47]

Myrdal abstained from making specific recommendations with respect to how the racial problem should be solved. 'He regarded social engineering as the "supreme task of social science"'.[48] He saw his task in *An American Dilemma* as laying the analytical groundwork for a new social policy

[43] Ibid., p. 1022.

[44] Jackson (1990, p. xi).

[45] Barber (2008, p. 64).

[46] Sowell (2011, p. 443).

[47] Ibid., p. 445.

[48] Myrdal kept coming back to this issue. Space limitations do not permit any exhaustive investigation here. However, his opening address at the Conference of the British Sociological Association in 1953 (Myrdal 1958) summarizes much of his thought on the issue. There he traced the changes in the position of the social sciences vis-à-vis policy making: the relation of social theory to social policy. Before the First World War, the social scientists 'were neither the final authors nor the executors of social policy' (ibid., p. 15). They were confined to academia, which, according to Myrdal, they developed rapidly. Their influence on social policy was due to their exposition of their thoughts and theories. With time, however, notably with the Great Depression, their role changed (ibid., p. 24):

rather than proposing particular legislation or outlining new policies in detail'.[49] Still,

> *An American Dilemma* exerted a powerful influence on American intellectuals, the educated reading public, and policymakers for twenty years after its publication. Myrdal's book played a key role in the campaign against disenfranchisement and segregation in the South; it convinced many whites that modern social science supported racial equality; it framed the question as a moral issue; and it helped to build some support for social engineering to lift the mass of blacks out of poverty.[50]

Not only that; the rest, as is well known, is history. In his very detailed book about *An American Dilemma*, especially about the reactions to it and the aftermath of its publication,[51] David Southern stresses the importance of Myrdal's work in court decisions: 'By 1954 Myrdal's name had become a household word in the halls of justice'.[52] The most famous case in which *An American Dilemma* was cited was *Brown v. Board of Education of Topeka*, the same year in the Supreme Court.

> In the institutional setup of modern democracy ... a function most important for its survival and growth falls on the social scientists: the long-range intellectual leadership thrusting society forward to overcome primitive impulses and prejudices and to move in the direction of rationality. Our independent status should not be merely a personal pleasantness and distinction; it should be used as a basis for exerting influence over the development of the thinking of the general public which fixes the limits to the freedom of the journalists, awards conditional power to the politicians and allows them to decide upon the policies which set the frame for the craftsmanship of the civil servants.

Myrdal explicitly refers to the social scientists as 'engineers of social policy', a function which he expected to grow more important in the future (ibid., p. 25). This, he stated, would serve to break down the borders between the traditional disciplines, since real-world problems did not accept such boundaries. He also cautioned against the feedback upon the social sciences themselves. The scientists risked bring coopted, and possibly corrupted, by the political power structures and their academic freedom risked being impaired.

[49] Jackson (1990, p. 187).

[50] Ibid., p. 310. For extensive accounts of the reception of *An American Dilemma* in the United States, see Southern (1987) and Jackson (1990).

[51] '... the tremendous amount of writing about race in the two decades after the *Dilemma's* publication is intimidating' (Southern 1987, p. 189).

[52] Ibid., p. 128.

> In the historic *Brown* case of 1954, Chief Justice Earl Warren declared that segregated schools harmed black children. As evidence for this crucial assertion, the chief justice, speaking for a unanimous Supreme Court, alluded to 'modern authority.' Warren specified this authority more fully in the controversial footnote 11, in which he cited seven social science studies. The famous footnote concluded with the words: 'And see generally Myrdal, *An American Dilemma* (1944).'[53]

The Supreme Court decided that school segregation was unconstitutional,[54] and two years later, racial segregation in buses was outlawed. Myrdal's role in these and similar events was beyond doubt:

> Hope sprang forth like flowers in spring with the integration of the armed forces, the Supreme Court's ruling on the desegregation of schools, the sit-ins, the freedom rides, and the first significant civil rights legislation in Congress since Reconstruction.[55]

Altogether, 'The numerous racial breakthroughs after 1944 elevated Myrdal to the status of a prophet in his own time'.[56]

An American Dilemma remained the most influential work on the American race issue for two decades. However, during the 1960s, things changed. Myrdal's analysis began to be questioned and the approach across the political spectrum to the race issue increasingly differed from the path laid out by Myrdal:

> By the end of the sixties ... many scholars concluded that Myrdal had been excessively optimistic about the power of education to reduce prejudice and that he had overlooked many psychological strategies that whites could use to adhere formally to the general principles of the American creed and still practice many forms of racial discrimination. Most scholars rejected Myrdal's formulations about the pathologies of black culture as inadequate for understanding the complex social and cultural life of poor blacks.[57]

[53] Ibid., p. 127.

[54] Jackson (1990, p. 124).

[55] Southern (1987, p. 189).

[56] Ibid.

[57] Myrdal (1944a, p. 928) had argued that '*American Negro culture is not something independent of general American culture, It is a distorted development, or a pathological condition, of the general American culture*', and he assumed that it was to the advantage

> Myrdal's assimilationist assumptions clashed with the desire of many blacks to define a distinctive Afro-American cultural identity. Liberals had moved beyond Myrdal's idea of equality of opportunity to advocate new forms of social engineering designed to produce equality of results, while radicals argued that the whole system had to be changed.[58]

Among the latter were many blacks. The civil rights movement had become less assimilationist and more verbally aggressive, with the insistence on 'black power', the emergence of such groups as the Black Muslims and the Black Panthers, and spontaneous urban black riots far from the non-violent approach of Martin Luther King, but the mainstream was affected as well. 'Every civil rights victory seemed to make blacks more impatient. As the movement became more inclusive and massive, it became less civil', writes David Southern.[59]

Challenge to Affluence

In 1962, Gunnar Myrdal came back to the problems of the United States, in a book called *Challenge to Affluence*.[60] There he noted that an 'underclass' was developing rapidly in the country.

of blacks, both as individuals and as a group to be assimilated into the culture of the dominant white group. This amounted to a misunderstanding of black American culture and its expression. 'With respect to jazz, for example, Myrdal was tone-deaf' (Barber 2008, p. 81). He was a square who played the lute (Andersson 1989, note, p. 16). Had he been hip he would not have missed Billie Holiday's rendition of *Strange Fruit*, written by the Jewish school teacher Abel Meeropol, a song about lynching, recorded in 1939 for the legendary Commodore label:

> *Southern trees bear a strange fruit*
> *Blood on the leaves and blood at the root*
> *Black bodies swinging in the southern breeze*
> *Strange fruit hanging from the poplar trees ...*

The story of the song is told in Margolick (2000). The tune is available, e.g., on Classic 601: *Billie Holiday and Her Orchestra 1939–1940*.

[58] Jackson (1990, p. 310).

[59] Southern (1987, p. 236).

[60] Myrdal (1962b).

> ... changes [...] are under way to trap an 'under-class' of unemployed and, gradually, unemployable and underemployed persons at the bottom of a society, while for the majority of people above that layer the increasingly democratic structure of the educational system creates ever more real liberty and equality of opportunity, at least over the course of two generations.[61]

Myrdal made it clear that the number of people (millions) who risked falling into abject destitution was decreasing as a result of increasing productivity and improvements in the educational system. This coin, however, also had a reverse side. New production methods called for better education across the board, i.e. also among those at lower echelons in the job hierarchy. 'This process has continued steadily downwards, first to middle positions and then to ever lower strata of employees in industry and commerce, until it is now beginning to make unskilled and many skilled workers redundant'.[62] However, following the logic of circular, cumulative causation, the very poverty of the bottom strata excluded them from education and hence pushed them deeper into poverty and permanent unemployment.

> They will become disheartened and apathetic. As parents they will not be able to pay toward such support of the education of their children that would be needed. Instead, they will have an incentive to take them out of school early if any employment, even at low wages and promising no secure future, offers itself. The home environment of the unemployed and poor will generally be less conducive for children and youth to become educated and trained for good jobs.
>
> The unemployed will be forced to live in the slums or, more probably, they will always have lived in the slums. Whatever the regulations are, the schools will be bad in the slums as they will be in the districts where the backwoods farmer lives. And the whole way of life in the crowded slum quarters in the cities or the rural slum districts will be destructive for the will and ability to advance in life.[63]

[61] Ibid., p. 34.

[62] Ibid., p. 37.

[63] Ibid., p. 42.

The poor in the United States were 'the least revolutionary proletariat in the world'.[64] They were not well organized and hardly participated in the election process. Many belonged to minority groups. '... the Negroes are still "the last hired and first fired"'.[65] Their unemployment rate was three times the average. Myrdal calculated that more than one-fifth of all Americans were poor in 1960. 'There is an ugly smell rising from the basement of the stately American mansion'.[66]

Again, Myrdal's solution of the poverty problem may be described as a piece of social engineering. He argued that in order to achieve full employment in a sustained way, investment in education, training and retraining of workers must be made an integral part of the strategy. Economic growth and reduction of poverty had to be aimed for at the same time. In order to stimulate aggregate demand, large-scale redistributive reforms were urgently called for. '*Never in the history of America has there been a greater and more complex identity between the ideals of social justice and the requirements of economic progress*'.[67]

This twofold expansion, in turn, required comprehensive long-range planning where all the plans for particular areas were integrated into an overall plan for the entire economy:

> Once America has decided that it wants to inaugurate a policy leading to rapid and steady economic growth, this implies the necessity of long-range economic planning. There will always be questions to answer: growth *of what* and *for what*, and growth *at what cost* – in the latter respect, not only economically but in terms of changing institutions and human relations in case they do not all go in the desired direction and are not part of the growth that is aimed at.[68]

Myrdal's approach was ambitious, to say the least:

> [The] various strands of government policy do not fall into place in the big puzzle without detailed planning in all the various fields: public construction work, spatial and vocational reallocation of the labor force, education,

64 Ibid., p. 43.
65 Ibid., p. 44.
66 Ibid., p. 49.
67 Ibid., pp. 64–65.
68 Ibid., p. 83.

> training and retraining, social security of different types, changed taxation on the federal, state, and municipal level, agricultural policy, wage and price policies, and so on. New drafts of city plans and transport systems will have to be produced.[69]

Myrdal was completely convinced of the power of planning.

[69] Ibid., p. 84.

CHAPTER 5

The International Dimension of Poverty

Gunnar Myrdal returned to his native Sweden from the United States in 1942, but already the following year, he was back for a few months as financial counselor at the Swedish embassy in Washington, DC. His task was to study the situation of the United States, the country's future prospects and its planning efforts. Upon returning home once more, in 1944, he published a book which became slightly notorious, *Varning för fredsoptimism* [Beware of Peace Optimism],[1] because he predicted a likely depression during the coming years—a prediction that turned out to be completely erroneous. The same year, he again became a member of the First Chamber of the Swedish parliament and was appointed chairman of the Swedish Commission for Economic Postwar Planning, a commission which he dominated to such an extent that it became popularly known as 'the Myrdal commission'.[2]

[1] Myrdal (1944b).

[2] For an extensive discussion of the work of the commission and Swedish economic policy during Myrdal's term as Minister of Trade, see Appelqvist (2000).

M. Lundahl, *The Dynamics of Poverty*, Palgrave Studies in the History of Economic Thought,
https://doi.org/10.1007/978-3-030-73347-6_5

Minister

In 1945, upon the dissolution of the wartime government of national unity, Gunnar Myrdal became Minister of Trade, a position which he had to leave in 1947, after a series of unfortunate events for which he was blamed by the public opinion. It began with the decision of the Riksbank, initiated by Myrdal,[3] to revalue the Swedish krona on July 11, 1946, to dampen cost increases and neutralize inflationary tendencies emanating from the United States. The revaluation, however, led to increased imports in a situation where the balance of trade already displayed a deficit and to a drain of the foreign currency reserves over the next six months.[4]

This was followed by a speech by Myrdal to the Swedish Economic Association [Nationalekonomiska Föreningen] on 3 December where he revealed that the government was contemplating the introduction of quantitative import restrictions. The speech provoked strong reactions from Prime Minister Tage Erlander and Myrdal's predecessor as Minister of Trade, Bertil Ohlin, who both in their memoirs blamed him for having increased imports and triggered an accelerated outflow of currency. However, as Örjan Appelqvist has demonstrated, Myrdal's speech only had a minor impact.[5] Nevertheless, the conventional wisdom had it that the speech was a blunder and that he was responsible for an accelerated outflow.[6]

The third event was the conclusion of a trade agreement with the Soviet Union which included sizeable export credits. The deal, which on the one hand aimed at guaranteeing a market for Swedish exports and on the other hand at helping the Soviet Union to rebuild its economy

[3] Myrdal (1982, p. 229).

[4] The revaluation led to a loss of 658 million dollars between 9 July 1946 and 28 January 1947. The total loss of dollars and gold during the same period was 1,390 million (Appelqvist 2000, p. 498). These figures must be seen against the background that 97 percent of the Swedish trade balance deficit was due to the trade with the North American continent.

[5] The real drain on the currency reserve did not take place until the end of January 1947, during a Swedish party leader conference, and after a letter from the board of the Riksbank (Central Bank) which argued that it was impossible to postpone import regulation measures. Between 28 January and 25 February 1947, 120 million US dollars were lost (two-thirds of the remaining dollar reserves) (ibid., pp. 268–79).

[6] Example, Lundberg (1956, p. 7) and Gustafsson (1987–1989, p. 155).

after the war and which had been initiated by the government of national unity, triggered a press campaign which Örjan Appelqvist calls 'one of the most vehement press campaigns ever after the second world war'.[7] The business community was hostile to the deal, in spite of the fact that it had been actively involved in its initiation. In the vulgar debate whatever was wrong with the Swedish economy was blamed on it. The Swedish workers were the ones who would have to foot the bill. Myrdal was—unfairly—held responsible for the contents of the agreement, which in some circles were seen as the initiation of a complete dependency of the Swedish economy on the Soviet Union. In the end, the Social Democratic government, however, simply concluded what the government of national unity had initiated.[8]

Fairly or unfairly, Myrdal had to resign as minister. It was not just a question of factual matters. As Ernst Wigforss succinctly expressed it,

> … it was part of Myrdal's nature not always to make the distinction between circles and situation where playfulness had its place, and those where it might be perceived as uncertainty with respect to your own point of view or shifts under the influence of moods. It may be said that intellectual talents of the rare kind exemplified for example by Gunnar Myrdal do not have any place in practical policy as designed e.g. in our own country. […] It is possible that those are right who contended that he did not really fit into the Swedish political climate.[9]

Geneva

In 1947, Gunnar Myrdal became the executive secretary of the newly established United Nations Economic Commission for Europe (ECE) in Geneva—the first regional organization of the UN.[10] The idea behind the organization, which was commissioned by the Economic and Social Council (ECOSOC), was to 'seek a comprehensive approach to the reconstruction of war-torn Europe and counteract the forces that were

[7] Appelqvist (2000, p. 368).

[8] For details, see ibid., pp. 367–84.

[9] Wigforss (1980, pp. 362, 364).

[10] For Myrdal's ECE activities, see e.g. Jackson (1990, pp. 320–32), Angresano (1997, pp. 70–78), Barber (2008, pp. 97–110), Rivarola and Appelqvist (2011), and Appelqvist (2014, pp. 63–68).

splitting Europe into two blocs'.[11] Things did not turn out that way however, but Myrdal found himself fighting against interests that were not intent on unity at all:

> On March 12, 1947, President Truman had asked Congress for $400 million in economic and military aid to the governments of Greece and Turkey, and on June 5, Secretary of State George Marshall announced that the United States would launch its own program of economic assistance to war-torn Europe. Myrdal lobbed energetically with American, British, French and Soviet diplomats to establish an aid program for the whole of Europe, administered by the ECE, but his efforts met with resistance on several fronts.[12]

The Marshall Plan operated independently of the ECE. Its aim was not to develop all of Europe but to keep the Western European states free from communist influence and to create a market for American export goods there. The communist states were as suspicious as the Americans. They were reluctant to provide information about their economies and they feared to be outvoted by the West. All of this made it difficult to work according to the original intentions of the ECE. The coordination of the American aid was carried out first by the Conference of European Economic Cooperation, which met in Paris in 1947, and from 1948, by a new body: The Organization for European Economic Cooperation (OEEC).

The East-West split in Europe left the ECE in a bit of a vacuum, but Myrdal tried to live up to the original intentions by facilitating trade between the two blocs in Europe and by providing quarterly surveys of the economic problems of Europe. He did what he could to preserve the independence of the ECE and establish an organization with a first-rate staff. This was not easy, since the risk of politicization was always lurking around the corner:

> Myrdal was to confront two models regarding the role of an international bureaucracy when setting up his 200-strong staff: the first was to view its officers as representatives of member countries; the second was to consider them independent civil servants, whose loyalty would be to the

[11] Jackson (1990, p. 321).

[12] Ibid., pp. 322–33.

> UN Charter and the task allotted to them by ECOSOC. Should considerations of realist power politics prevail, or the liberal universal ethos of the UN Charter? Myrdal did not hesitate to pursue a recruitment policy based on scientific merit, even if it was at odds with opinions within influential governments.[13]

He managed to put together a first-class team, whose members were responsible to the ECE rather than to their home governments. Myrdal tried to depoliticize as much as possible of the work of the ECE. His team included Nicholas Kaldor from the London School of Economics as head of the research and planning division, Walt W. Rostow from Harvard, P. J. Verdoorn from Holland, Kaldor's former student Tibor Barna, Ester and Mogens Boserup from Denmark, and Ingvar Svennilson, the director of the Institute for Economic and Social Research [Industriens Utredningsinstitut (IUI)] in Stockholm, who wrote his masterly *Growth and Stagnation in the European Economy* there.[14] The ECE team produced analytically first-rate, professionally independent economic surveys which provided important inputs to the public discussion of the economy of post-war Europe.

Myrdal also managed to break down some of the barriers against East-West trade in Europe. This was by no means an easy task, for as much as 40 percent of the pre-war trade volume was subject to embargoes—because of the military importance of the goods—which reached their peak in 1952–1953.[15] But he managed to have an impact:

> Myrdal's greatest contributions during his decade at the ECE were his effort to encourage East-West trade and his attempt to promote détente before it was fashionable in Washington and Moscow. Many of his plans were blocked during the early years of the ECE by Western trade embargoes designed to deny the East bloc industrial products and materials that might aid in the expansion of its industrial and military power. Tensions rose during the Korean War, and both sides obstructed plans put forth by Myrdal and the ECE Secretariat. With the end of the Korean War boom, however, Western business leaders in need of new markets began to look toward the East bloc, and the Western governments reduced their 'strategic

[13] Rivarola and Appelqvist (2011, p. 37).

[14] Svennilson (1954).

[15] Adler-Karlsson (1968, p. 143).

> trade' controls. By 1954, East-West trade increased substantially, and the Soviet Union and the Eastern European countries began participating more fully in ECE committees. The structure that Myrdal developed at the ECE was to prove useful as the superpowers gradually replaced brinkmanship with détente.[16]

What Myrdal achieved was no mean feat. 'That he managed to set a structure in place for planning European economic recovery and promoting intergovernmental cooperation at the height of the Cold War was a remarkable achievement'.[17]

The International Economy

Gunnar Myrdal also spent much of the 1950s working on problems related to poverty and inequality on the international level and on the relation between polarization between regions within a country and polarization between countries. This resulted in a 'trilogy': *An International Economy*, *Development and Under-Development: A Note on the Mechanism of National and International Economic Inequality*, usually referred to as his Cairo lectures, and *Economic Theory and Under-Developed Regions* (or *Rich Lands and Poor*).[18]

An International Economy had its origins in a keynote speech that Myrdal gave on the occasion of the bicentennial of the foundation of Columbia University in New York in May 1954. The theme that had been assigned to him was 'Toward a More Closely Integrated Free-World Economy'. During the remainder of 1954, this speech was expanded into a full-fledged monograph on the state of international economic relations outside the Soviet bloc: *An International Economy*.

In this book, Myrdal, the internationalist, began by lamenting the lack of international integration and noting the trend toward greater international inequality. For him, international economic integration meant the realization of '*the old Western ideal of equality of opportunity*'.[19] The richer countries were progressing while the poorer ones were either stagnating or retrogressing. This had been the case for several generations.

[16] Jackson (1990, pp. 323–24).

[17] Ibid., p. 331.

[18] Myrdal (1956a, 1956b, 1957a, 1957b).

[19] Myrdal (1956a, p. 11).

Neither international migration, capital movements nor trade had been able to overcome this trend. 'Immigration from the poorest regions, with the largest amount of surplus labor, is excluded in almost all receiving countries by statutory or administrative color bars'.[20] The underdeveloped countries were receiving extremely little private capital from abroad, but private investment was not their primary need:

> What the underdeveloped countries need most of all … so as to proceed with their development plans, is capital for large-scale investment in public utilities: railroads and highways, electric power stations, irrigation, port facilities, and the like. With the possible exception of electricity, these are not usually profit-making enterprises and they will have to be owned and operated by the state or public authorities. Formerly, investments of this kind in backward countries were often financed by loans raised in international markets, but it is exactly that type of private capital import which is no longer forthcoming.[21]

The attitude in Wall Street toward Third World countries was not favorable, and unfortunately, public capital flows did not make up for the shortfall. Myrdal argued in favor of increased international aid. Bilateral capital flows would not do, since they were strongly influenced by all kinds of political considerations on part of the donors. 'Only by insulating … the ultimate receiver of financial aid from the contributor will it to some extent be possible to remove the political element from this international redistribution of resources, or at least keep to a minimum elements of demagogy, log-rolling, and pressure politics'.[22]

International trade, in turn, did not at all have the properties that orthodox trade theory postulated. Above all, it did not lead to any factor price equalization. '… instead of an equilibrium, as the theory of international trade would demand, we are facing *a cumulative process away from equilibrium in factor proportions and factor prices, engendered by international trade …*'[23]

[20] Ibid., p. 93.

[21] Ibid., p. 108.

[22] Ibid., p. 124.

[23] Ibid., p. 225.

Dreams and Realities

The main problem of the poor countries was their lack of internal integration, which in turn made their bargaining power in the international arena weak. Myrdal was dreaming of a 'world government' which could work to further the interests of the poor:

> When international integration is held as an ideal, the corresponding political image, carried to its logical perfection, is a world state under a world government, directed by a democratic process in which, directly or indirectly, all people participate. Such a world government would have good reason to instigate policies which, viewed from the *status ex ante* position, discriminated in favor of the great majority of backward peoples.[24]

A world government, however, was nowhere to be found. The countries of the Third World had to pen their own development strategies, and development was not just a matter of economics. Myrdal observed that the economic progress of the advanced countries had gone hand in hand with profound changes in the social fabric. These interacted with economic development:

> ... the gradual attainment of national integration had its essential base in these noneconomic changes: increased social mobility both locally and within the entire national community, which opened up the avenues for competition and individual advance; intensified social cohesion and practical solidarity in the nation as a whole, which formed the basis for the coming into force of rules that applied to the entire community and for the sharing within the whole nation of the burden of common expenditure; increased participation of all the citizens, on local and national levels, in the political responsibility of controlling the social processes. It was through such changes that greater equality of opportunity was gradually attained. Economic development was in many ways a driving force, but it was itself made possible and continuously sustained by all the other socially integrating forces.[25]

[24] Ibid., p. 4.

[25] Ibid., p. 169.

The need for social change was even more pressing in the contemporary underdeveloped countries, where the social structures were frequently rigidly closed:

> When economic change hits a society of such closed minds and entrenched social rigidities, social values are destroyed almost of necessity. It cannot be expected to embark more or less as a matter of course upon an almost automatic process of adjustment to economic changes which, by their cumulative repercussions on all social factors, will carry it through the early industrialization phase towards our modern welfare state of mutual solidarity and commonly shared high living standards. *To prepare the way for economic development such countries need institutional reforms of the social structure on a vast scale*; without them the only result will be an end of the security and solidarity of the stagnant, isolated, local social compartments.[26]

Such changes entailed redistribution of incomes and wealth. Myrdal called for land reform and progressive taxation, educational reform and a health care system that did not simply cater to the rich. He also stressed the importance of a population policy that served to reduce birth rates. Otherwise, the advances in medicine that served to reduce death rates would simply increase poverty and human suffering. The development program also entailed a proper balance between efforts in different sectors. Development was not tantamount to just industrialization. Increasing productivity in agriculture served not only to increase the incomes of poor peasants, but also to create a market for domestically produced manufactured goods.

The poor countries needed a proper commercial policy, and Myrdal analyzed it from the point of view of their interest. He advised them to maximize the value of their exports, since the ability to export determined the ability to import the capital goods that were necessary for their development effort. These countries were exporters of primary goods, usually not more than one or two, which in turn raised the question of the long-run development of the price of these goods vis-à-vis that of manufactures as well as the issue of price fluctuations calling for stabilization schemes. No international agreement existed with respect to these two issues. The solution recommended by Myrdal was diversification of

[26] Ibid., p. 171.

exports, into goods with high income elasticities of demand, if possible manufactured goods. The latter was not an easy task, however, since it meant competing with the efficient producers in the already industrialized countries. Possibly, economic integration among poor countries could do something to widen their markets, but little had been achieved in practice. A diversification also entailed increased use of capital goods, which had to be imported. This made it necessary to restrict imports of non-essential goods, notably luxuries, which called for interventions in the market mechanism. The accumulation of domestic capital, in turn, made it necessary to restrict domestic consumption. Higher standards of living could be achieved mainly in the longer run, since they rested on the creation of more production capacity.

The Cairo Lectures

In October 1955, Gunnar Myrdal gave the National Bank of Egypt Fiftieth Anniversary Commemoration Lectures in Cairo. The lectures were published as a book the following year.[27] The theme he chose was that of national and international inequalities, a theme which of course was intimately related to the poverty issue, and which he had also dealt with in *An International Economy*. His point of departure was once more 'the very large and steadily increasing economic inequalities between developed and under-developed countries'.[28] The per capita income of the latter was only a fraction of that of the former and some of these countries had even moved backwards.

Myrdal wanted to explain the pattern that he observed and again resorted to his idea of circular, cumulative causation.[29] The traditional theory of international trade, in his view, could not explain the disparities. It was conceived in terms of stable equilibrium and pointed to equalization of incomes. Instead, Myrdal suggested, the analysis would have to concentrate on the quality of the factors of production and the effectiveness of their use in different lines of production. The notion of stable equilibrium was false. The economic system is '*not steering towards such a*

[27] Myrdal (1956b).

[28] Ibid., p. 7.

[29] Based on Myrdal (1957a), Toner (1999) inserts Myrdal's view of cumulative causation into a comparative historical perspective.

position at all but, rather, is continuously en route away from it'[30] in the cumulative fashion sketched in *An American Dilemma*.

Myrdal's claims were extraordinarily strong: 'I have suggested that the principle of interlocking, circular interdependence within a process of cumulative causation has validity over the entire field of social problems'.[31] Referring, first, to the problem of regional differences within a country, he stated that the market mechanism normally would cause inequality, not equality. It would cluster economic activities in certain localities while leaving the rest of the country in a backwater. The expanding regions would attract migrants from other areas and capital would flow there as well. The same was true with respect to trade, and industries would be concentrated in the richer regions while the poorer ones would remain agricultural. So would infrastructure, including health and education. All this constituted what Myrdal first termed backsetting effects, later changed to backwash effects, in an extended version of his lectures, *Economic Theory and Under-Developed Regions* (the British version) or *Rich Lands and Poor* (the American version),[32] which is the term that we will use here.

Myrdal, however, did not exclude the possibility of development in certain regions. Against the backwash effects he set 'spread effects':

> It is natural that around a main centre of expansion a whole surrounding region is more or less taken into the stride as it becomes spurred ahead by increasing outlets of agricultural products and stimulated to technical advance and rational business conduct all around. There is also another line of 'spread' to localities farther away, where favourable conditions exist for producing raw materials for growing industries. These and all other localities, where new starts are being made and happen to succeed, become in their turn, if the expansionary momentum is strong enough to overcome the Backsetting Effects, new centres of self-sustained economic expansion.[33]

However, the spread effects tended to be weak: the weaker the poorer the country. They were a function of the level of development and their

[30] Myrdal (1956b, p. 18).

[31] Ibid., p. 25.

[32] Myrdal (1957a, b).

[33] Myrdal (1956b, p. 31).

relative weakness contributed to the maintenance of the vicious spiral in underdeveloped countries. In richer countries, on the other hand, they were strong enough to push the development process:

> A high average level of development in a country is followed by improved transportations and communications, higher levels of education and a more dynamic communion of ideas and values, which all tend to strengthen the forces for the spread of economic expansion. [...] sustained and rapid progress becomes an almost automatic process when a country has once reached a high level of development.[34]

The cumulative process will not run forever. Malthusian checks on the growth of the population, via increased death rates, are likely to provide a brake on the fall of the living standard (possibly counteracted by advances in medicine which reduce death rates so as to increase the misery). At the other end of the income scale, industry may become too concentrated and generate external diseconomies of congestion with concomitant cost increases. With an almost Marxist twist, Myrdal also suggested that demand may be slackening in a 'maturing' economy, which in turn may require new markets or increased government expenditure. Factor prices may increase to the point where the established regions find it difficult to compete with emerging ones.

Myrdal also introduced the state into his scheme of circular, cumulative causation. In the richer countries the welfare state had been introduced to a varying degree, and this in turn served to improve the lot of the poor and reduce the extent of regional inequality. Richer regions have to pay for this. 'In the poorer countries, on the other hand, market forces have been given a relatively freer play, when their effects to create regional inequalities have not been actually supported and magnified by built-in feudal and other inegalitarian institutions and power structures aiding the rich in exploiting the poor'.[35]

[34] Ibid., pp. 32–33.

[35] Ibid., p. 37.

International Inequalities

Myrdal next moved from interregional to international income disparities. '... on the whole, in recent decades the economic inequalities between developed and under-developed countries have been increasing'.[36] On the international level as well, he argued, trade acts to widen the income gap instead of making it close. Trade had destroyed the handicraft sectors in many poor countries by flooding the latter with cheap imports, promoting instead the exports of primary commodities which meet an inelastic demand in international markets as well as strong price fluctuations. In addition, the strong population growth in poor countries had created a large supply of cheap labor which in turn tended to make the fruits of technical progress in the export branches accrue to the importer countries in the form of low prices while the wage level in the exporting countries remained low. Capital movements would not provide any solution to this dilemma, since by and large, investors tended to prefer to put their money into the already developed countries:

> After the collapse of the international capital market in the early 'thirties, which has not been remedied, and later the breakdown of the colonial system, which had given security to the foreign investor, it would almost be against nature if capital in large quantities were voluntarily to seek its way to under-developed countries in order to play a role in their economic development.[37]

Myrdal did not deny that international trade and transportation could generate spread effects in underdeveloped countries, but these effects, he claimed, would largely be limited to the export-import ports and their immediate surroundings. This would result in isolated enclaves rather than in a chain of positive effects extending into the regions.

Myrdal did not think much of the possibility of reducing international inequalities through international organizations. The latter were weak and toothless, 'in the main only propaganda fora and, in addition, media for diplomatic contacts between governments and for consultations'.[38]

[36] Myrdal (1957a, p. 6).

[37] Myrdal (1956b, p. 50).

[38] Ibid., p. 58.

Instead, he recommended poor countries to resort to a rational nationalism, taking '*any and all measures which, on the ground of good reasoning, can be proved to enhance its own economic welfare*'.[39] He did so 'with a clear conscience' that such an approach 'would bring us nearer, and not further away from the stage when an integrated world policy, based on international solidarity, could with more effectiveness be attempted'.[40] The bargaining power of the poor nations was weak, but, Myrdal thought, it could be improved somewhat by cooperation between them.

The Need for National Strategies

The development strategy had to rest on a national development plan. 'It is now commonly agreed that an under-developed country should have a national economic development policy. Indeed, it should have an overall, integrated national plan, as is also urged by everybody', wrote the convinced social engineer.[41] The intrinsic deficiencies in poor countries made it necessary for the state to assume a number of functions which in developed economies could be left to private business. In particular, it had to ensure increased investment. Like most other economists in the mid-1950s, Myrdal felt that the road to economic growth and development went through increased capital formation:

> There is no other road to economic development than a forceful rise of the part of the national income which is with-held from consumption and devoted to investments, and this implies a policy of utmost austerity – so independently of whether the increased savings are engendered through high levels of profits to be ploughed back in industrial expansion or through increased taxation.[42]

The alternative to this heroic attempt was continued economic and cultural stagnation or retrogression.

When it came to the plans themselves, Myrdal argued that they could not be conceived in terms of the prevailing or expected market prices, since the latter provided no indication of the future needs of the economy,

[39] Ibid., p. 59.

[40] Ibid., p. 60.

[41] Ibid., p. 62.

[42] Ibid., p. 64.

in particular when it came to large, indivisible infrastructural investments that were to ensure the viability of industries that would be created only in the future. Market prices could not handle external economies. The plans would have to be political documents and welfare would have to be defined by the political process. Myrdal therefore called for a blueprint in real terms of the entire process of cumulative causation that would lead up to the desired future result.

> A whole cumulative process has to be blue-printed in terms of concrete investment projects and their effects: on the volume of production in various lines, on consumption, on the employment of workers and natural resources, on health, education and the productiveness of labour, and so on, in various sectors and in different years, with main attention focused on the circular causal interactions between all the factors in the system. The plan must also determine the concrete state interferences to be applied to the markets in order to assure that the process really comes off and develops as planned.[43]

Myrdal was completely aware that this was not easy: 'I stress the need that the plan should be founded on study, and indeed study of some of the least accessible functional relationships in the social system: namely the coefficients of circular causation between all the factors in the system'.[44] No objective criteria that could guide the planning process were available. On the contrary, the choice of ends and means was a policy choice 'reached in terms of national development goals as determined by the political process'.[45]

As he had demonstrated in *An International Economy*, Myrdal was under no illusion that the politico-administrative equation was an easy one to solve. The 'perfect' state regularly assumed by planning advocates was not to be found in the poor countries. The entire administrative machinery would have to be set up more or less from scratch:

> Underdeveloped countries have to attempt to create an efficient and honest political and administrative machinery without much in the way of legal

[43] Myrdal (1957a, p. 88).

[44] Ibid., p. 86.

[45] Ibid., p. 89. Cf. also the discussion of ends and means in Myrdal (1958, Chapter 10), originally published in German in 1933.

traditions. And time does not allow them a purgatory era of economic liberalism; *they have to reform their politics and their administration at the same time as the state is increasingly compelled to handle vast public funds and run business on a large scale.*[46]

The International Dimension

The planning principle applied to international trade as well. Myrdal called for a dynamic theory of comparative costs and he considered that underdeveloped countries could request unilateral trade liberalization in developed countries, 'on rational grounds'.[47] 'The theory of international trade and, indeed, economic theory generally were never worked out to serve the purpose of explaining the reality of economic underdevelopment and development'.[48] Traditional economic theory built on the notion of stable equilibrium, a notion which in Myrdal's eyes was completely unrealistic. In addition, it limited the attention to 'economic' factors, which he thought was entirely mistaken. '… it is useless to look for one predominant factor, a "basic factor", such as the "economic factor"'.[49] Instead, economic and non-economic factors interacted in a circular, cumulative fashion, internationally as well as interregionally.

The skepticism with respect to the traditional theory of international trade applied in particular when it came to the imports of capital goods necessary for the creation of a manufacturing industry. If these were larger than what the country's exports allowed, imports of consumption goods must be restricted in order to create room for the necessary strategic imports. This required government intervention in the pattern of international trade. Myrdal also invoked the infant industry argument. Protection of local industries would give the latter a chance to compete in the domestic market and grow.

Nationalism and restrictions on international trade should, however, not be allowed to be carried too far. In *Beyond the Welfare State*, from 1960, Myrdal cautioned that while many countries in the Third World were characterized by internal dissension and leaders hence had to push

[46] Myrdal (1956a, p. 204).

[47] Myrdal (1956b, p. 74).

[48] Myrdal (1957a, p. 9).

[49] Ibid., p. 19.

for national integration and cohesion, the process could easily derail and degenerate. The national feelings could easily be turned outwards: against foreign nations and nationals:

> The politicians can thereby easily bring themselves to a position where they are virtually compelled to take policy steps against foreign interests which are not motivated by the country's true development interests, but only by the intense nationalistic feelings amongst the people, which must be satisfied if they are to retain power.[50]

Finally, Myrdal commented on the need for technological change. The 'one advantage' that these countries had was 'our accumulated scientific knowledge', upon which they could draw.[51] This knowledge, however, could not be used as a simple blueprint, but the receiving countries would have to adjust and accommodate techniques through independent research so that they suited their own values and conditions.

Beyond the Welfare State

A few years later, Gunnar Myrdal published yet another book which dealt with planning: *Beyond the Welfare State*, 1960. There, the emphasis is on planning in the Western democracies and in the Third World.[52] The latter were in a situation that differed substantially from that of the former. 'Indeed', writes Myrdal, 'it is very unlikely that they will develop much, or at all, if the state does not take a much bigger responsibility for engendering development, than was taken by the state during the industrial revolution in Western countries'.[53] This, in turn, had consequences for the role and timing of planning:

> By the very logic of the under-developed countries' situation, planning becomes programmatic in its approach. [...] In the under-developed countries, the idea precedes its realization. As economic development cannot be expected to come by itself, planning becomes a precondition for development, not, as in the Western countries, a later consequence of development

[50] Myrdal (1960, p. 158).
[51] Myrdal (1956b, p. 76).
[52] Myrdal (1960).
[53] Ibid., p. 88.

> and all other changes which accompanied it. The under-developed countries are thus compelled to undertake what in the light of the history of the Western world appears as a short-cut.[54]

In the Third World, according to Myrdal, planning had to anticipate public policy making. 'It does not grow out of the necessity to coordinate such policies as have already been initiated'.[55] Planning even had to encompass the 'building up of institutions for self-government, collective bargaining and cooperation',[56] since in stagnant societies, these institutions did not come into existence spontaneously.

Criticism

Myrdal's views of international inequality and poverty met with strong criticism from mainstream economists. A.D. Knox wrote a short but effective review of *Economic Theory and Under-Developed Regions* in *Economica*.[57] He found the book interesting and stimulating but was far from convinced by Myrdal's argumentation technique. Knox thought that he exaggerated and that the choice of the terms spread and backwash effects was emotional. Neither 'rich' nor 'poor' countries were homogeneous groups. It was not in any way obvious that all underdeveloped countries were falling behind the rich ones.

Knox questioned Myrdal's analysis of the impact of international trade. The fact that trade had not been a powerful agent of growth did not necessarily mean that it had contributed to stagnation and impoverishment. Also, it did not seem reasonable to claim that the 'free' play of market forces had a negative impact on the underdeveloped countries. Markets in those countries were frequently anything but 'free' and the proper role of state intervention was not that of a substitute for the market but governments in underdeveloped countries should work *with* the market, creating an environment that would allow the market forces to work as freely and efficiently as possible.

[54] Ibid., p. 89.

[55] Ibid., p. 90.

[56] Ibid., p. 98.

[57] Knox (1960).

In an even shorter review in the *Journal of Political Economy*, Gerald Meier (1959) concentrated on Myrdal's criticism of conventional economic theory and his own substitute for it. Meier's opening line is strong indeed: 'This [*Rich Lands and Poor*] is the most provocative, and in some respects the most provoking, book yet written on the development problems of poor countries'. He thought that Myrdal went too far in his attacks. 'Indeed, the criticisms may appear at times almost to caricature economic theory …'[58] Meier did not give much for the concept of cumulative causation. It was nothing but an unstable equilibrium, and the use of spread and backwash effects was not original either. Harvey Leibenstein's 'income-raising' and 'income-depressing' forces and Albert Hirschman's 'trickling-down' and 'polarization' effects expressed the same idea.[59] It made no sense to counterpose cumulative causation and negative effects of international trade to the traditional factor price equalization theorem and income convergence, since the latter theorem was never intended to be an adequate description of reality.

In two journal articles published the year before (1958), Meier provided a more extensive criticism.[60] He was careful not to put Myrdal into the vulgar, Marxist, camp. In the first article, he wrote:

> In supporting his contention that international trade has operated as a mechanism of international inequality, Myrdal does not appeal to any simple notion of deliberate exploitation of the poor countries by foreign

[58] Meier (1959, p. 636). See also Meier (1963, Chapters 6–7).

[59] Leibenstein (1957, Chapter 8) and Hirschman (1957). The latter, in a comparison between the two pairs of concepts noted (Hirschman, 1958, note, p. 187) that

> … there are considerable differences in emphasis and conclusions. Myrdal's analysis strikes me as excessively dismal. In the first place, he fails to recognize that the emergence of growing points and therefore of differences in development between regions and between nations is inevitable and is a condition of further growth anywhere. Secondly, his preoccupation with the mechanism of cumulative causation hides from him the emergence of strong forces making for a turning point once the movement toward North-South polarization within a country has proceeded for some time. Finally, the picture that he paints of international transmission of growth is also too bleak in my opinion as he overlooks that the polarization (backwash) effects are much weaker between nations than between regions within the same country.

[60] Meier (1958a, b).

> investors or foreign governments; Ricardo is not crudely confronted with Lenin. Instead, in a more sophisticated manner, Myrdal believes that international market forces have been unfavourable for the poor country by creating a highly unbalanced economy and by causing a secular deterioration of the terms of trade.[61]

Meier took issue with the idea that protection of industry would improve the economic situation of underdeveloped countries. These countries, according to Myrdal himself, were countries with an unbalanced, dualistic, structure, where a small industrial, often foreign-dominated, sector, usually in plantations or mining, not integrated with the rest of the economy, had been superimposed on a traditional, mainly agricultural sector, which had created an export bias in their economies. However, primary export products were subject to deteriorating terms-of-trade, and Myrdal hence proposed protection of the domestic industrial sectors of the developing countries.

Meier questioned the view that the unbalanced structure of the economies of underdeveloped countries were actually due to the operation of international forces and instead argued that it may be caused by limited domestic investment and narrow domestic markets, forces that biased foreign investment toward the export enclave sectors. He contended that Myrdal concentrated too much on his criticism of the factor price equalization theorem with its unrealistic assumptions, e.g., that of identical production technologies in all countries. The real world did not exhibit the same characteristics as the Heckscher-Ohlin model framework.

Meier also criticized the idea that the terms-of-trade of underdeveloped countries were undergoing a secular deterioration. The available calculations suffered from several defects, like the choice of base year, the non-inclusion of new products and declining transport costs, and even if the simple commodity terms-of-trade did undergo a deterioration, this to an unknown extent could be counteracted by productivity increases, and in the end, the trends of the past may be misleading when it comes to predicting the future.

Meier concluded that 'much of Myrdal's analysis does not rest on solid historical and analytical foundations, and … the notions of disguised unemployment and a secular deterioration of the terms of trade are much

[61] Meier (1958a, p. 277).

too ambiguous to support the policy conclusion of protection'.[62] His recipe for progress differed sharply from Myrdal's, notably in its views of the role of foreign trade:

> The remedy does not lie in policies of protection and deliberate industrialization at the expense of agriculture and foreign trade. Instead it depends on the promotion of these domestic conditions – particularly in the political, social, and institutional framework of the economy – that will permit the expansion of the export sector to induce secondary changes in the domestic sector. If this is accomplished, foreign trade might then also serve the poor countries as an 'engine of growth'.[63]

Meier's second article (Meier 1958b) dealt specifically with Myrdal's views of the trade policy of developing countries as exposed in *An International Economy*. He took issue with the latter's argument that there are 'four special reasons for industrial protection in underdeveloped countries – the difficulties of finding demand to match new supply, the existence of surplus labor, the large rewards of individual investments in creating external economies, and the lopsided internal price structure disfavoring industry'.[64]

According to Meier, Myrdal failed to provide any valid reasons why import substitution would be superior to other patterns of industrialization, he did not provide any quantitative indications of the type of commercial policy required and he assumed that the necessary capital and entrepreneurship would be forthcoming automatically. He did not offer any evidence that surplus labor did in fact exist, and even if it did, it could not be taken for granted that industrialization based on protection would be the best way of absorbing it. Myrdal furthermore simply assumed, without proof, that the external economies realizable by import substitution would be larger than those forthcoming by investment, e.g., in exports or infrastructure. Finally, a price policy designed to favor industry would discriminate against agriculture and exports, both of which were essential ingredients in any development strategy.

The most devastating criticism came from P. T. Bauer, a pro-market, pro-trade, anti-state intervention economist with a strong libertarian

[62] Ibid., p. 288.

[63] Ibid., p. 289.

[64] Myrdal (1956a, p. 279).

bent.[65] He contended that Myrdal's international trilogy was disappointing. It provided little new knowledge and few new insights. Bauer thought nothing of Myrdal's contention that economic concepts tend to be value loaded and of his effort to make value judgments explicit:

> This argument is unacceptable. The principal concepts of economics are not value loaded: for example, concepts of opportunity cost, demand and supply as functions of price, the volume of output or of imports and exports, the consumption function and the multiplier, and the devices of aggregation, general and partial equilibrium analysis and period analysis; contrary to Professor Myrdal's assertion, neither these concepts or methods, nor their usefulness, depend on political valuations.[66]

Myrdal simply failed to make the distinction between positive and normative economics. The validity of the propositions of the former is entirely independent of political judgments. Bauer argued that Myrdal confused the advancement of knowledge with the promotion of policy, which in turn made it impossible to reach agreement 'even on elementary propositions'. 'Such a position destroys economics as a systematic discipline'.[67]

Bauer objected to the use of circular, cumulative causation as the general mechanism. This makes it impossible to break out of poverty without the aid of external forces and is contradicted by the historical experience of both the developed countries which began as underdeveloped and the countries in for example south-east Asia which were beginning their development at the time when Myrdal was writing. Myrdal furthermore offered no evidence for his contention of the increasing inequality between developed and underdeveloped countries. In Bauer's view, he confused low incomes and stagnation.

Myrdal's view that the contact between developed and underdeveloped countries had contributed to the latter's plight was considered erroneous by Bauer, who argued that the historically politically independent countries in Africa and Asia were 'among the most backward, usually much more so than the neighbouring ex-colonies'.[68] Nor did Bauer accept the argument that foreign-dominated enclaves in underdeveloped economies

[65] Bauer (1959), extended version: Bauer (1971b). I will refer to the latter.

[66] Bauer (1971, p. 449).

[67] Ibid., p. 450.

[68] Ibid., p. 456.

did not serve to improve the position of the latter. On the contrary, they generated government revenues, spread skills and promoted the monetary exchange economy.

Myrdal's picture of underdeveloped countries as rigid, economically and socially highly stratified societies won no acceptance either. Bauer thought of them as consisting of masses of 'materially undifferentiated people'[69] and when incomes were unequal, this was usually not a result of inherited wealth or government favors but the inequalities were 'bound up with differences in economic faculties, such as perception of economic opportunity, industry, thrift or persistence, unrelated to special privileges or institutional or monopolistic restrictions'.[70] Men are not equally endowed by nature and inequalities do not constitute an obstacle to economic development.

Needless to say, Bauer did not find any redeeming features in Myrdal's insistence in the necessity of comprehensive planning, especially not since it did not rest on the use of the price mechanism and disregarded costs. It did not take individual choice into account. The only opinion that counted was that of the government, which Myrdal confused with the national interest. Nor did Bauer agree with Myrdal's insistence on transfers from rich to poor countries without conditions. How could such transfers be a moral obligation if the use of the funds and the policies pursued were not taken into account?

Bauer's final judgment was that Myrdal's triple effort was unscientific: 'These books are concerned with the promotion of policy instead of the promotion of knowledge'.[71]

[69] Ibid., p. 459.

[70] Ibid., p. 460.

[71] Ibid., p. 470.

CHAPTER 6

The Culminating Effort: *Asian Drama*

When Gunnar Myrdal left the Economic Commission for Europe, in 1957, he embarked upon a mammoth study that would keep him busy for a decade. This study was what would become *Asian Drama*—a work that dealt with Pakistan, India, Ceylon, Burma, Malaya, Thailand, Indonesia and the Philippines, and to a lesser extent, Cambodia, Laos and South Vietnam.[1] It was originally intended to be completed in two and a half years' time, but things did not turn out that way, naturally enough, for Myrdal's approach and perspective were grandiose: in the end 2,284 pages. The work was a natural successor to both *An American Dilemma* and the works on international economic issues of the previous decades, since it centered on poverty. Well aware of the attention it would receive, its author did not hesitate to give it the subtitle *An Inquiry Into the Poverty of Nations:*

> It is not altogether a pretentious metaphor when I describe my endeavor to supply an institutional approach in this study as an attempt to analyse the development problems of South Asia in the manner that Adam Smith studied England's development problems two hundred years ago.[2]

[1] Myrdal (1968).

[2] Ibid., p. x.

M. Lundahl, *The Dynamics of Poverty*, Palgrave Studies in the History of Economic Thought,
https://doi.org/10.1007/978-3-030-73347-6_6

The Theme

The extent of poverty, not only in South Asia, but in all the ex-European colonies, was overwhelming. In a lecture given at Wayne State University in Detroit in May 1963, Myrdal stated:

> ... I do not hesitate to state that the large masses of these peoples live in the most abject poverty, with a standard – in all conceivable ways – which is so low that people in the rich countries are hardly capable to imagine. And this standard is not improving, at least not with any noticeable speed. The income gap between the rich and the poor countries of the world, which has grown during a hundred years, is now growing faster than ever.[3]

The absolute situation of the poor nations was even worse. The slow development in the countries that displayed any progress at all had slowed down even further, and in the rest of them stagnation, or even retrogression, was the rule. Domestic social and economic inequalities loomed large and very few effective reforms had been carried out to change this sad fact. The political development of the poor countries was not necessarily positive. Many of them had entered the road toward more authoritarian government, frequently with army backing. Myrdal argued that it would be impossible to forecast where they would be five years henceforth. His conclusions breathed pessimism:

> *We are probably entering a very critical period in the history of the underdeveloped countries.* They will feel increasingly disillusioned in their efforts to bring about economic development. Several of them will suffer a deterioration of the general standard of living, especially for the vast majority. Radical changes may occur in the form of government and the political system of these countries, and you have to reckon with numerous conflicts between neighboring countries. At least in some parts of the underdeveloped world the political development will not proceed in the direction that we would desire.[4]

This was the theme that Gunnar Myrdal would extend and develop in *Asian Drama*, the work that brought his methodological tenets and the poverty issue to their logical climax. There he merged the five

[3] Myrdal (1964, p. 25).

[4] Ibid., pp. 31–32.

pillars that had grown in his mind since the late 1920s: explicit value premises, dynamic analysis, institutionalism, circular, cumulative causation and social engineering. 'I found myself engaged in a study where the main concern was methodological – how to cleanse concepts and discard theories and then state problems in a logical and realistic way ...'[5]

The three volumes of *Asian Drama* on the one hand deliver a formidable critique of the approaches that characterized contemporary thinking on development economics and on the other hand attempt to put together an approach that leaves no stone unturned, no connection unexplored. The attempt is overly ambitious, not to say overambitious, ranging from a mapping of economic and social conditions in eleven South Asian countries, through a circularly causal, historical, analysis of how their contemporary parameters (attitudes and institutions) had evolved—'The writer knows of no instance in present-day South Asia where religion has induced social change. Least of all does it foster realization of the modernization ideals'[6]—to a call, based on explicitly stated value premises, for physical dynamic planning, encompassing most of society, to bring about change in a cumulative fashion. Never was Gunnar Myrdal more institutional than in *Asian Drama* and never was he more acerbic in his judgment of conventional wisdom. As he puts it himself, 'If the book has any degree of originality, it is as a total composition and in the insistence upon following the basic institutional approach through to its consequences'.[7]

An Institutional Approach

Myrdal presented what he thought of as very good reasons for approaching the poverty problem of South Asia in institutional terms: 'We shall use as a starting point the incontrovertible fact that the basic social and economic structure of the countries of South Asia is radically different from that existing in advanced Western countries'.[8]

[5] Myrdal (1968, p. xi).

[6] Ibid., p. 103.

[7] Ibid., pp. xii–xiii.

[8] Ibid., p. 26.

> Not only is the social and institutional structure different from the one that has evolved in Western countries, but, more important, the problem of development in South Asia is one calling for induced changes in that social and institutional structure, as it hinders economic development and as it does not change spontaneously, or, to any very large extent, in response to policies restricted to the 'economic' sphere.[9]

In spite of the fact that the economists had 'always been the cavalry of the social sciences' and had been the ones 'spearheading the attack on the dynamic problems of underdevelopment, development, and planning for development',[10] Myrdal called for interdisciplinary research.

He provided it too. *Asian Drama* is nothing less than a kaleidoscope of South Asia and its problems. It covers all conceivable aspects. The work is divided into six different main parts, each one long enough to constitute a book on its own: political problems, economic realities, planning, labor utilization, population size and population quality. In each, Myrdal mapped, in as much detail as the scant statistical material permitted, the prevailing situation, the factors that had caused it, the indigenous forces calling for change, not least nationalism, with its own dynamics, and the main events that had taken place after independence, politically, country by country, economically, topically arranged, population and its utilization in the different sectors of the economy, the structural division of the economy as well as the evolution of the economy as a whole, living standards and inequality, size and composition of foreign trade and capital movements and, finally, differences in initial conditions.

Asian Drama is heavy on methodology. It contains no less than sixteen appendices concerned above all with criticisms of the conventional wisdom of development economics, ranging from the use of models in general, to the inapplicability of the Western economic terminology in the South Asian context, but Myrdal also set out his own approach to the mechanisms behind underdevelopment and development and to economic planning. Exactly like in *An American Dilemma*, his view of the world of South Asia rested on the notion of circular, cumulative causation:

> We conceive of the situation in each South Asian country – as in any other country – as a *social system*. The system consists of a great number of

[9] Ibid.

[10] Ibid., p. 28.

conditions that are causally interrelated, in that a change in one will cause changes in the others. We classify the conditions in six broad categories:

(1) output and incomes;
(2) conditions of production;
(3) conditions of living;
(4) attitudes towards life and work;
(5) institutions;
(6) policies.[11]

All these conditions influence and are influenced by each other. '… *the movement of the whole social system upwards is what all of us in fact mean by development*'.[12] In the same way as in *An American Dilemma*, a change in any of the six conditions will trigger changes in the others in a cumulative fashion.

There is a big difference between *An American Dilemma* and *Asian Drama*, however. In the former book, Myrdal argued that once the cumulative process had been set in motion there were no forces that would act so as to push the system back toward its original position. In *Asian Drama*, he allowed for factors that may act as a brake on cumulation or even ensure that the cumulative process does not begin. 'Normally', he noted, 'one might, on purely theoretical grounds, think that the social system would regularly be moving in one direction or another since impulses to change would be continually fed by circular causation with cumulative effects'.[13] However, this is not what is likely to be observed in the real world:

> In sharp contrast to this expectation are not only the common experience of 'low-level equilibrium' in underdeveloped countries and the serious obstacles to development policies, but more generally the astonishing stability of most social systems in history. Balance, far from being the fortuitous result of an unusual and obviously unstable combination of forces, seems to be the rule, not the rare exception. The great bulk of historical, anthropological, and sociological evidence and thought suggests that social stability and equilibrium is the norm and that all societies, and underdeveloped societies in particular, possess institutions of a strongly stabilizing

[11] Ibid., pp. 1859–60.
[12] Ibid., p. 1868.
[13] Ibid., p. 1871.

> character. In view of these findings the real mystery is how they can escape from equilibrium and can develop.[14]

Myrdal made a distinction between three types of forces that make for stagnation: time and inertia (mainly attitudes and institutions), independent counteracting forces (e.g., population growth) and counteracting forces released by development (like soil erosion produced by increased agricultural production). For a cumulative process to be set in motion, it is not enough that the factors composing the social system interact. The strength of the interaction must be large enough and the speed of the reactions must be high.

Social Engineering Once More

In *Asian Drama*, Myrdal again insisted on social engineering. Ideally, planning would proceed in steps. First, adequate knowledge of the relevant conditions, their causal connections and their coefficients of change is to be gathered. Second, a set of adequate value premises to guide the planning process in a direction that allows for an upward movement on all counts must be chosen. The actual value premises used by Myrdal in his study were all related to the desire of modernization, essentially along Western lines, of the South Asian societies: rationality, development and planning for development, rise of productivity, rise of levels of living, social and economic equalization, improved institutions and attitudes, national consolidation, national independence, political democracy, democracy at the grass roots, social discipline and 'democratic planning'.[15] This would, in turn, allow the planners to choose the appropriate policies.

Myrdal was of course aware of the formidable requirements that had to be met in order to produce an ideal or optimal plan. 'There is no need to stress the impossibility of gaining even a fraction of that full knowledge of conditions and their causal connections. Some of the significant data needed are among the most inaccessible social relationships, still largely unknown even in Western countries …'[16]

[14] Ibid.

[15] Ibid., Chapter 2.

[16] Ibid., p. 1880.

Still, he insisted, planning constituted the only rational way of breaking out of the traditional society. To approximate and simplify was a time-honored scientific practice and it should be applied to planning as well, even in situations where the fact base was scant. If we divide the forces at work into two groups, factors promoting development or underdevelopment on the one hand, and the standard of living or level of development on the other, Myrdal's account indicates that the South Asian societies were caught in a stable equilibrium at a low level of development as a result of the interaction of the two kind of forces, and that efforts to break out of this equilibrium would have to be of a magnitude large enough to overwhelm the forces that promoted underdevelopment. Some kind of 'big push' was required that would bring the social system beyond a new, unstable, equilibrium at a higher level of development with stronger development promoting forces. Failure to do so would simply push the system back to the original position, whereas moving beyond the unstable higher equilibrium would create a virtuous spiral that would in its turn end in yet another—high-level—equilibrium of the stable kind.

The above has implications for planning. As Myrdal expressed it: '*There is economy in the big push.* Smaller efforts mean waste. The effectiveness of the push depends, of course, not only on the size of the efforts but also on their timing and direction'. For the planning effort to be efficient, 'not only … the efforts have to be larger than a critical minimum, but also … *directed simultaneously at a great number of conditions, concentrated within a short period of time, and applied in a rationally coordinated way*'.[17] It is not enough to concentrate on planning in economic terms but the necessary change of non-economic variables must be tackled as well.

Furthermore, Myrdal thought that the planning must be carried out in physical terms, since the employment of the prevailing market prices would be of no use in a situation where it came to tracing the cumulative interaction of economic and non-economic variables over time.

> … *all effective planning is physical planning*. Financial and fiscal planning is at best a reflection of physical planning. Physical planning is exceedingly difficult, and rough estimates and guesses are necessary, particularly in countries with an extreme scarcity of knowledge of the relevant facts. The practice of presenting the plan as a financial plan has several flaws.

[17] Ibid., p. 1901.

> First, it tacitly assumes that finance is the only bottleneck and that physical resources flow smoothly, at constant unit costs, in the direction indicated by money expenditure. Secondly, even if the financial or fiscal plan is given the more modest role of merely reflecting an underlying plan that coordinates physical magnitudes, it is impossible to avoid the implicit assumption that all of the obstacles to development can be overcome by a sufficient expenditure of physical resources and that, even where non-physical obstacles exist, the effectiveness of policies to remove them is related to resources used up in the process. Neither assumption is justified in the countries of South Asia.[18]

Myrdal devoted six chapters of *Asian Drama* to a discussion of planning. His point of view was that of the social engineer:

> The basic principle in the ideology of economic planning is that the state shall take an active, indeed the decisive, role in the economy [...] The whole complex ideology of planning, in all its manifestations, is ... essentially rationalist in approach and interventionist in conclusions. It is committed to the belief that development can be brought about or accelerated by government intervention.[19]

Myrdal traced the spread of the planning ideology in South Asia and its relation to nationalism, egalitarianism and democracy. He then went on to discuss planning in four countries where socialism was the official political creed: India, Ceylon, Burma and Indonesia, noting that state ownership and management was contemplated, 'if at all', only in a limited number of instances: public utilities, large-scale industry, mines, large plantations, banking, insurance and 'to some extent' commerce.[20]

Another chapter was devoted to 'democratic planning': in the first place, the active participation of the masses in the preparation and implementation of plans but also the requirement that this participation should be voluntary. The rationale is simple. Without changes in the way people think and act no development will take place. People must 'alter their attitudes toward life and work ... and cooperate to improve society and its institutions'.[21] Unfortunately, Myrdal had to conclude: 'The structure on

[18] Ibid., p. 1923.

[19] Ibid., p. 709.

[20] Ibid., p. 808.

[21] Ibid., p. 851.

which the South Asian countries are trying to build democratic planning is in general weak and inimical to development: it reflects the stagnation and underdevelopment from which they are trying to escape'.[22] The issue of voluntariness was particularly difficult. According to Myrdal, there was little hope for rapid development in South Asia without greater social discipline throughout society, all the way down to the village level, which would not be achieved without regulations backed by compulsion, but the entire institutional and attitudinal structure worked to block such regulations. In addition, the South Asian states were 'soft states', in the sense that they required

> ... extraordinarily little of their citizens. There are few obligations either to do things in the interest of the community or to avoid actions opposed to that interest. Even those obligations that do exist are enforced inadequately if at all. The low level of social discipline is one of the most fundamental differences between the South Asian countries today and Western countries at the beginning of their industrialization.[23]

The use of plans also called for operational controls of the private sector: positive or negative, discretionary or non-discretionary. This posed a dilemma. Private ventures were desirable and had to be supported by the authorities, but adherence to the planning ideology had often led to the adoption of far too many administrative discretionary controls. India was a case in point:

> The fact is that *no major and, indeed, few minor business decisions can be taken except with the prior permission of the administrative authorities or at the risk of subsequent government disapproval.* This means that 'private' business is something entirely different from what it normally is in the Western countries ...[24]

Furthermore, regulations call forth attempts to avoid them, which in turn calls for more regulations, etc. In the end, an 'odd situation' was created, where *most officials have to devote most of their time and energy to limiting or stopping enterprise*. This is like driving a car with the accelerator pushed

[22] Ibid., p. 859.

[23] Ibid., p. 896.

[24] Ibid., p. 921.

to the floor but the brakes on'.[25] The situation produced other undesirable results as well. Those enterprises which succeeded in maneuvering among the—mainly discretionary—controls could reap extraordinarily high profits, in a situation characterized by monopolies, oligopolies and vested interests—a situation that would frequently degenerate into sheer corruption.

Underutilization of Labor

Asian Drama is an exercise in criticism, but not exclusively. The 'constructive core' of the work deals with the use and quality of the human factor. As Myrdal saw it, the main reason for underdevelopment and poverty in South Asia was the underutilization and the low productivity of the labor force:

> An extreme underutilization of labor is generally assumed to characterize South Asian countries. That there is fundamental truth in the assumption is suggested by the obvious fact that the average output of the labor force is very low. It is partly low because much of the labor force is idle, either completely or for a large part of the day, week, month, or year. But even when members of the labor force are at work, their productivity is usually low. This phenomenon can only be explained as the result of many conditions, among them low labor efficiency.[26]

Myrdal questioned the validity of such 'Western' terms as unemployment and underemployment, especially in the context of agriculture. In industrialized countries, the unemployed wanted to work and macroeconomic policies that stimulate aggregate demand could be used to increase employment. In South Asia this was far from always the case. The fundamental fact was that labor was underutilized, either because it was idle or because, when working, it produced very little, and macroeconomic measures could do very little to change this fact. Other factors were responsible:

> Instead, the bulk of the labor force is embedded in a climatic, social, cultural, and institutional matrix that not only tends to perpetuate present

[25] Ibid., p. 925.
[26] Ibid., p. 961.

> low levels of labor utilization, but also resists rapid and immediate adaptation to novel and unfamiliar ways of living and working. Idleness and low labor efficiency depend upon institutions, custom and tradition, attitudes toward work and leisure – including taboos and inhibitions related to status and to the participation of women in work. Moreover, the relevant attitudes are set in a framework of institutions, and the relationship between attitudes and institutions is mutually reinforcing.[27]

In this situation, it makes no sense to analyze the situation in terms of involuntary unemployment. Myrdal instead proposed an approach that centered on labor utilization. He focused on three ratios: participation (the number of working members in the labor force), duration (the number of hours worked per working member) and labor efficiency (the output per man hour worked). The conventional Western wisdom deals only with the first of these ratios ('employment') but neglects the other two.

Myrdal proceeded sector by sector, from traditional agriculture to the non-agricultural sectors. He provided an account of how agricultural institutions and behavior evolved in South Asia and the consequences for labor utilization. '… the social and institutional environment of traditional agriculture places a high premium on abstention from productive work'.[28] Participation rates were low and falling, the duration of the work year was shortened by holidays and ceremonies, and incentives to put an effort into the work were lacking. 'There is no situation where income and levels of living could not be improved substantially by a larger and more intensive labor input'.[29] The situation was self-perpetuating.

The non-agricultural sectors in South Asia were small in comparison, but Myrdal nevertheless devoted a fair amount of attention to them, since he considered them less tied to tradition and custom and hence more amenable to contribute to the effort to break through the constellation of factors that kept South Asia in poverty. Here as well he condemned the mechanical use of the employment-unemployment dichotomy. Although less forcefully, the same type of mechanisms as those prevailing in traditional agriculture were at work in those sectors.

[27] Ibid., pp. 999–1000.

[28] Ibid., p. 1070.

[29] Ibid., p. 1092.

The most interesting of them was the manufacturing industry. Myrdal held that it was impossible to increase incomes without industrialization, especially since the populations of the South Asian countries were growing rapidly. To rely on exports of manufactured goods was difficult. The world market was not easy to penetrate. Therefore, these countries had chosen to fall back on import substitution in the domestic markets. Their markets were, however, small. In addition, the typical pattern was that import substitution had been generated by a strained foreign exchange situation. The development of manufacturing required imports of capital goods, so the substitution usually took place in the less 'essential' markets for consumer goods, which were afforded protection. The latter type of goods was hardly those that would contribute the most to the planned development recommended by Myrdal.

The choice of techniques posed yet another problem. While the South Asian countries could in principle draw on the accumulated technical knowledge developed in the West, techniques there had been developed in a situation of labor scarcity, whereas in Asia labor was abundant. However, even using labor-intensive techniques, the industrial sector would not be able to absorb large numbers of workers. It would simply be too small for that in the foreseeable future, and agriculture would have to continue to bear the brunt of the rapid population growth. The spread effects generated by manufacturing were likely to be weak and geographically concentrated.

> ... clearly, industrialization in this form is not enough to accomplish a significant change in the economic structure of these countries and to give real momentum to development. Indeed, if not accompanied by direct interventionist policies toward other sectors of the economy, it would merely bolster the enclave pattern of colonial economic experience.[30]

For Myrdal, there was no way around social engineering and planning. 'What these countries need is a program that will induce changes simultaneously in a great number of the conditions that hold down their

[30] Ibid., p. 1204.

growth; fundamentally, the task of the planners is to coordinate all of these changes in such a way as to spur development'.[31]

Modern and Traditional Sectors

The case for industrialization rested heavily on the modernization ideals. These ideals were, however, not shared by everybody. A rival ideology existed, which had to be reckoned with:

> Traditionalists of all shades ... share several convictions. They believe that village crafts should be encouraged, that measures should be taken to promote self-sufficiency at both the village and the national level, and that modern industrial products – particularly imported consumer goods – should be viewed with suspicion.[32]

Acknowledging the fact that the 'traditional ideology' would not easily go away, Myrdal examined the 'rational reasons' for supporting village crafts on the one hand and modern small-scale industry on the other. In the former case, it would be necessary to increase productivity by the provision of improved tools and simple machines and well as to improve the organization of production and marketing. Part of the solution, however, lay outside the cottage industry sector. The main market for such goods was found in the agricultural sector and the extension of it hence depended critically on improvements of production and increased incomes there. Protection would also be required, Myrdal argued, since most of the craftsmen had no alternative employment.

Small-scale industry—industries larger than family enterprises, using hired labor—was a different matter. They could be used to decentralize industrialization and required less capital than large-scale firms. When Myrdal wrote *Asian Drama* not much had, however, been accomplished in South Asia, and especially not when it came to balancing the different types of industrial establishments against each other:

> ... the South Asian countries face the problem of achieving a balance between large and small production units. It would be very unfortunate to have an economy consisting of a few big enterprises and a vast multitude

[31] Ibid., p. 1205.

[32] Ibid., p. 1208.

> of farms and craft enterprises; under the level of big industry there should be a layer of smaller industrial enterprises.[33]

Ideally, large and small industries should complement each other. Small firms could deliver inputs to large firms and work as service establishments to the latter and they could also obtain some of the inputs they used to produce finished goods from the large-scale sector. Like the craft sector, the small-scale industries, however, did not have their fate entirely in their own hands, and unless they could export, advancing across a broad front required increased domestic incomes that led to a widening of the market.

Myrdal did not see any immediate modernization of industrial production in South Asia: 'The case for protecting and promoting the craft industries in the villages of South Asia is a strong one, particularly in the poorer countries', he wrote. The lack of alternative employment made this the only way of improving the productivity and income of the village craftsmen. By the same token, however,

> … the preservation and promotion of cottage industry in the villages, and a similar type of policy toward agriculture … implies that the underdeveloped countries of South Asia will have two distinct sectors: a small, but gradually growing, fully modernized sector of large-scale and small-scale manufacturing enterprises and a vastly larger sector that will use labor-intensive techniques not too different from the traditional ones and continue to give work to most of the rapidly increasing labor force. And as the modernized sector will economize on labor and will not create much employment for a long time to come, while the labor force will grow rapidly until the end of the century, this pattern cannot be merely a transitional one; it will have to be accepted as the pattern that will prevail for many decades.[34]

Myrdal cautioned, however, against leaving the traditional part of the economy to its time-honored practices. Both agriculture and crafts should be induced to adopt modern, more productive, techniques, 'but these should be deliberately chosen to take account of the present vast underutilization of labor and the rapid growth of the labor force'.[35] This, in turn, called for fresh research on labor-intensive technology able to

[33] Ibid., p. 1223.

[34] Ibid., p. 1239.

[35] Ibid.

absorb more of the growing labor supply. Concentrating planning just to the construction of large-scale industry and leaving traditional pursuits to their fate was 'to invite failure on a grand scale'.[36]

Modernization of Agriculture

The last component in Myrdal's call for a better labor utilization was the elaboration of an agricultural policy. Agriculture was the most important sector of the economy. 'Fundamentally, it is in this sector that the battle for long-term economic development in South Asia will be won or lost'.[37] Even though statistics were lacking, it was obvious that the underutilization of labor in agriculture was substantial. Many did not work, or worked very little, and when they worked, they did not produce much. The traditional institutions stood in the way of a rational use of the agricultural labor force—a serious problem, especially given the high rate of population growth.

To increase agricultural production was an issue of supreme importance. Food imports were increasing since domestic production failed to keep pace with the growth of the population, in a situation where in most South Asian countries the calorie intake was already low. Yields were low, but Myrdal was hopeful that they could be increased with the aid of modern scientifically based agricultural technology and an increased labor input. '… *a fuller utilization of the labor force and a higher level of agricultural production are not only compatible objectives but, indeed, two aspects of the same thing*'.[38] Mere price increases would not do the trick, however, Myrdal argued, since much of the marketable surplus was extracted by moneylenders and landowners through mechanisms dictated by power and tradition.

The available statistics indicated that the cultivated land area could be more or less doubled, but much of the time, traditional social forces kept the land idle. Land reclamation had been slow also because schemes tended to be top-heavy and encourage waste and many schemes had not lived up to the political expectations. Conversion of grazing lands to cultivated plots was possible, through cultivation of fodder crops that allowed

[36] Ibid., p. 1240.

[37] Ibid., p. 1241.

[38] Ibid., p. 1255.

for a reduction of the former. Irrigation schemes had frequently been costly and peasants had failed to respond to them, either because they entailed changes incompatible with the traditional way of life or because they required an increased use of fertilizer. Production increases required the simultaneous change of a number of agricultural practices: new seed varieties, irrigation, fertilizer and possibly also mechanization. Technological reforms were exceedingly important, however, because they allowed an improved utilization of labor.

Agricultural change is not only a function of inputs and technology. As always, Myrdal stressed the importance of institutional reform. Land reforms had been undertaken only at a modest scale.

> The failure to emerge on radical land reform might … be understood in the light of the complexity of interests concerned with land tenure. The wide diffusion of land ownership even among the urban upper middle class and non-cultivators in the rural areas, both groups including many government servants in the lower as well as the higher ranks, creates a formidable anti-land reform bloc …[39]

Another necessary measure was the legal protection of tenant rights against the landowners: security of tenure and limitation of the share of the latter group in the harvest—a difficult undertaking, especially since the administration of such measures had been left 'to civil servants who often lack both the qualifications and the integrity necessary for the job and are overburdened with responsibilities'.[40] Cooperation among villagers to increase production and equality had also failed its purpose. Myrdal's verdict was harsh. It was an illusion to believe that the creation of cooperatives would increase equality. They simply did not attack the inegalitarian power structures. On the contrary, the latter frequently manipulated the cooperatives in order to benefit themselves, e.g., from government subsidies, with the result that the extent of inequality increased. Credit cooperatives did not serve the poorest, those with low creditworthiness. This group had to do what it had always done: turn to moneylenders who charged very high interest rates.

Community development efforts, 'a tremendously ambitious effort to spark a cumulative process of rural uplift in village societies encrusted by

[39] Ibid., p. 1303.

[40] Ibid., p. 1330.

centuries of stagnation',[41] inspired by an egalitarian spirit, had in practice tended to favor 'not only the wealthier residents within a village but also the wealthier villages and regions'.[42] The result was that the 'hopeful vision of a massive uplift throughout the rural population has clouded and such mass enthusiasm as the program occasionally managed to elicit in its earlier stages has largely faded'.[43] The efforts made to mobilize idle labor for projects that would benefit the agricultural communities in the villages had fared no better.

> Every effort to mobilize and organize underutilized labor for investment purposes has been a failure or near-failure. Cooperative farming was motivated partly by the belief that a consolidation of land would encourage investments that could not be undertaken by individual landowners ... the program of cooperative farming has been abortive.[44]

When Myrdal summed up the achievements of agricultural policy reform in South Asia after the Second World War, he was forced to conclude that, if anything, the situation in South Asian agriculture had deteriorated:

> Broadly speaking, the post-war attempts to reform the agricultural structure in South Asian countries have met with limited success; indeed, the record is strewn with disappointments. A reduction in the top layer of parasitic absenteeism has been accomplished partly in India. Nevertheless, many of the least desirable features of the traditional pattern of ownership rights and obligations have survived. Perhaps the most common result of post-war policies in India and other South Asian countries has been the strengthening of the upper strata in the villages and a corresponding reduction in the position of sharecroppers and landless laborers in the lower strata of rural society. All the significant measures for agricultural uplift adopted by the governments – whether technological or institutional – have tended to shift the power balance of the rural structure in favor of the privileged classes.[45]

[41] Ibid., p. 1339.

[42] Ibid., p. 1341.

[43] Ibid., p. 1342.

[44] Ibid., p. 1359.

[45] Ibid., pp. 1366–67.

The reason for this was not only the privileged power position of the upper echelons, but also the fact that these groups—peasant landowners and privileged tenants—responded eagerly to government incentives in the form of aid and technical assistance. 'Naturally, they have obtained more benefits than have other members of the agrarian structure who are apathetic and who have neither the means nor the incentive to avail themselves of the advantages offered'.[46]

Myrdal argued that for production to increase in the long run, it was necessary to promote social and economic equality:

> As long as working and earning an income jeopardize status while land-holding and partial or complete abstention from productive work raise it, aggregate output is held well below its potential. If, on the other hand, measures to reduce inequalities can succeed in removing deterrents to work, aggregate labor utilization and production may be simultaneously advanced.[47]

A very radical change in the approach to agricultural policy making was required, but Myrdal had little hope that this would materialize. The politicians were simply not responsive. Nevertheless, he set out to sketch some of the measures. His approach rested on a radical redistribution of land in favor of the actual tillers. Myrdal rejected the common argument that a redistribution would lead to reduced production because the new landowners would be less experienced than the former ones. The land was owned in large chunks but cultivated in small, in most cases by tenants who did not own it. If anything, the situation was the opposite one. Everyone was using more or less the same methods and would continue to do so. Sharecroppers were experienced cultivators—much more so than absentee landowners.

Myrdal was also skeptical to the argument that the new owners would lack capital. This could be overcome by a pooling of such things as draft animals and tools. And there was plenty of scope for increased labor efforts given the traditional techniques. Myrdal was convinced that the redistribution of land would provide an incentive to do a more careful job on the farm. By the same token, a radical land redistribution was likely to create a more receptive environment to technological change and

[46] Ibid., p. 1367.

[47] Ibid., p. 1369.

improved produce prices in the longer run. In the short run, on the other hand, the marketable surplus might shrink, since the part of the tenants' output that was formerly appropriated by landowners and moneylenders, and put on the market, would now be consumed on the farms.

Myrdal also saw another problem: that the traditional structures would take over, structures that hence would have to be wiped out. The main danger was that many new landowners would be indebted to moneylenders at the outset and that when their credit standing improved through the ownership of the land, they would be tempted to borrow more, mortgaging their land and in the end losing it. Myrdal therefore advocated a radical cancelation of old debts and a prohibition against moneylending, mortgaging and sales of land.

In spite of all the virtues that Myrdal saw in the radical land redistribution approach, he was, however, not quite convinced that it would do the trick:

> At best, a radical redistribution could ... only be thought of as a once-and-for-all change in the land tenure pattern, one that by virtue of its shock effect might cut through the obstacles to more intensive labor utilization that exist under the present system of inequalities. In view of the difficulties that we have enumerated, it appears that a radical land redistribution – despite its substantial merit in meeting the problem of dignity and status head on – does not even in theory represent a wholly favorable alternative to the *status quo*.[48]

Myrdal therefore also discussed alternatives to land redistribution. The first was radical land consolidation: nationalization of landholdings. This, in a setting of cooperatives, would make it easier to obtain an optimum farm size, doing away with the contemporary fragmentation and dispersion of the land and it would make it possible to realize the economies of scale inherent, e.g., in irrigation works. However, in order to be efficient, cooperative farming would require compulsory membership. Actual experimentation with cooperatives, with voluntary participation, had 'merely perpetuated the least favorable features of the existing system with all its inequalities in status'. It had 'failed to fulfill its promise'.[49] Soviet-type kolkhozes were also out of question because they were mainly

[48] Ibid., p. 1375.

[49] Ibid., p. 1376.

likely, as they had done in the Soviet Union, to create 'an embittered agrarian population more inclined to sabotage agricultural productivity than to advance it'.[50] Besides, their introduction would have to be preceded by a communist revolution.

In the end, however, Myrdal ruled out both radical land redistribution and radical land consolidation—as doctrinaire. 'With considerable hesitation',[51] he came out in favor of a third strategy that could be employed to break down the traditional status hierarchy which acted as a tremendous obstacle to a fuller utilization of labor, a strategy that turned some of his previous reasoning on its head:

> … the measures that have thus far been taken in the interest of agrarian uplift – land reforms, legal protection of tenants, cooperatives, community development programs, and agricultural extension services – have generally failed to accomplish their original purposes. But they have nevertheless had some impact, particularly in strengthening the position of the progressive peasant proprietors and privileged tenants. The elite group in the rural hierarchy has taken advantage of some of the new opportunities that governmental assistance has opened up, and it has reaped most of the benefits that have been distributed. Such increases in agricultural production as have occurred have undoubtedly been due in large part to the modernization peasant proprietors and privileged tenants accomplished with the help pf the government.[52]

What Myrdal suggested was to rely on these groups—'who possess the will and the capacity to respond to economic stimuli'—for the intensification and modernization of agriculture. Their potential for agricultural development had not been fully exploited and the more or less radical political discourse underlying the failed reform efforts had by and large made them uncertain with respect to their future fate. At the same time, the reform efforts had embarked upon a number of dubious equality ventures which in most instances had failed. 'The result', wrote Myrdal, is that agricultural policy has courted the worst of two worlds: equality has not in fact been promoted, with the result that people have

[50] Ibid.

[51] Ibid., p. 1378.

[52] Ibid., pp. 1378–79.

become discouraged and cynical, while efficiency has not been adequately recognized and rewarded'.[53]

Myrdal called on the governments to lay down a firm policy and see to it that it was implemented, and that policy should be a policy 'in favor of capitalist farming by allowing and encouraging the progressive cultivator to reap the full rewards of his enterprise and labor, while approaching the fundamental issues of equality and institutional reform from a different angle and by different policy means'.[54] A development path along these lines could not tolerate 'passive and parasitic land ownership on part of the persons who sap the surplus of the agricultural sector but contribute nothing to its productive performance'.[55]

To that end, Myrdal recommended a tax that heavily penalized landownership which was not combined with tilling the soil and the prohibition of land sales to non-farming non-residents. This amounted to '*a straightforward, practical line of reform*'.[56] A policy that proceeded along 'the controlled and restrained pattern of capitalist practice that has gradually evolved in Western countries' would 'create a climate in which efficiency could be more readily recognized and rewarded'.[57] It constituted a radical 'land reform' in the sense that landowners were encouraged to become cultivators and it would constitute a step toward the abolition of the sharecropping system. The scheme should also include the gifts of small plots of individually owned land to the poor landless to increase their income and to increase their incorporation into the market economy. Myrdal called his approach 'a modified form of welfare capitalism for agriculture'.[58]

In the end, however, Myrdal was pessimistic with respect to the future development of South Asian agriculture. He recognized that his suggestion would not be accepted by the politicians. They were likely to continue to propose allegedly egalitarian reforms without substantial content. At the same time, the vested powerful interests at the top of

[53] Ibid., p. 1379.

[54] Ibid., p. 1380.

[55] Ibid.

[56] Ibid.

[57] Ibid., p. 1381.

[58] Ibid., p. 1383.

the village structure would continue to do their best to frustrate genuine reform efforts.

> The most probable development in South Asian countries is undoubtedly a continuation of the present course. Under the banner of a 'social and economic revolution,' land reforms and other institutional changes of a radical character will be talked about and, occasionally, enacted into law in some form. Very little reform will actually be accomplished, and even greater inequality may result from both government policies and developments beyond government control, such as the increase of the labor force. A state of insecurity about the future of land ownership will be maintained that itself will tend to suppress improvements in production.[59]

A gloomy prediction indeed, for the sector that Myrdal considered central in the development process of South Asia.

Population Problems

The last two parts of *Asian Drama* are devoted to an analysis of population growth and population quality. The former deals with the population explosion that South Asia was subject to at the time and the causes behind it. Mortality was declining while fertility tended to remain constant and international migration had no significant effects anywhere in the region. The rapid population growth tended to increase the dependency burden of those in working age and to depress incomes since the modern sectors of the economies expanded only slowly. Both effects called for birth control measures '*as soon and as vigorously as possible*',[60] because, regardless of the effect on the population size, all measures to encourage a reduction of death rates had to be discouraged on ethical grounds. Myrdal emphatically stressed the need for birth control, since

> … the population explosion is the most important social change that has taken place in South Asia in the post-war era. It has been far more important than any reform or development efforts, and it has done a great deal to thwart these efforts. The possibility now exists that the spread of birth control will be the greatest change in the next few decades, gradually

[59] Ibid., p. 1384.

[60] Ibid., p. 1472.

> making reforms and development easier to accomplish. But whether the birth rates will decrease, and decrease rapidly, within the next decade must seem uncertain.[61]

The population question also had a qualitative aspect, summarized by Myrdal in terms of health and education. While education had attracted a strong interest among development economists at the time when he was writing, this was not the case with health. Myrdal objected. 'Poor health conditions are intimately linked with almost every aspect of life in South Asia', he bluntly asserted.[62] He surveyed the available statistics on mortality and morbidity, the health policies of the South Asian nations and the inequality of access to health facilities, linking health with climate, living standards (notably nutrition), sanitation and hygiene, and he noted the likely favorable effects of better health on productivity but also its tendency to increase the rate of population growth.

As far as education was concerned, Myrdal stressed that it had a double purpose:

> From a development point of view, the purpose of education must be to rationalize attitudes as well as to impart knowledge and skills. In the South Asian countries, which have largely been stagnant for a long time and where attitudes antagonistic to development have taken firm root and become institutionalized, the changing of attitudes requires far greater emphasis than in the developed countries, where attitudes are already more rational, and are adjusted to permit further rapid progress.[63]

Modern education was instrumental—indeed central—when it came to changing attitudes and institutions inimical to economic and social development. However, in South Asia it did not work quite that way. 'Throughout South Asia there is a traditional contempt for manual work and the educated tend to regard their education as the badge that relieves them of any obligation to soil their hands'.[64] This explained the phenomenon of 'educated unemployed', and it constituted a serious

[61] Ibid., p. 1530.

[62] Ibid., p. 1553.

[63] Ibid., p. 1621.

[64] Ibid., p. 1646.

obstacle to development. 'When schools of engineering and other technical training institutes were established, students commonly expected – and were expected – to become "deskmen"; and much the same attitude prevails today'.[65] While a Western engineer was prepared to use his hands, his Indian counterpart was not.

Myrdal stressed the importance of literacy—functional literacy—as an instrument for disseminating knowledge and for development in general. However, adult education had not been given any prominent place in the plans for educational reform in South Asia, and the lack of paper for printing reading material and paper to write on put severe obstacles to the process of advancing from minimum to functional literacy.

The formal school system displayed a number of deficiencies: repetition of classes, lack of attendance, high drop-out rates, low quality of teachers, low teacher salaries, low social status of teachers, overly theoretical curricula, lack of teaching materials—all of which had a negative impact on learning. The primary schools provided insufficient preparation for pupils going on to secondary education. Several languages and scripts had to mastered, with Western languages frequently taking precedence on higher levels. In addition, the school systems tended to preserve the traditional social hierarchy and stratification. The extent of vocational education was small, due not least to a lack of qualified vocational teachers, but not only that. The aversion to manual work also played an important role:

> The fact that vocational schools, even at the higher technical level, often require participation in manual work, which is despised, and that they presumably prepare students for jobs where manual work is part of the regular routine, helps make these schools less popular than the general ones. Although vocational schools are relatively so few, they often find it difficult to recruit students.[66]

Tertiary education had expanded in South Asia, but Myrdal found indications of considerable waste in the system: repetition and failure to graduate. Also, the allocation between different fields of study hardly matched either the demand situation or the needs posed by the development effort:

[65] Ibid., p. 1647.

[66] Ibid., p. 1762.

> Today most experts, South Asian and foreign alike, are of the opinion that these countries have an oversupply of 'generalists,' who have been trained in the humanities, law, and 'academic' science, and who swell the ranks of useless administrators, clerks, and the educated unemployed. At the same time, more engineers, agricultural technicians, doctors, dentists, pharmacologists, and, not least, teachers on all levels are needed.[67]

Although hard data were lacking, it also appeared as if the quality of university education was low, somewhere on the level of secondary education in most European and North American countries. The working and living conditions of the students were bad. Books, libraries and laboratory facilities were lacking; there was little contact with the teachers and guidance was minimal.

The entire educational system was selective, working in favor of the well-to-do and against the students coming from disadvantaged families. This was partly for economic reasons, but demand factors were responsible as well:

> These economic deterrents to the schooling of poor children operate in a social setting that in many other ways tends to perpetuate the upper-class monopoly of education. Since lower-class parents usually have had little or no education and are illiterate, they tend to have less interest in seeking an education for their children or in keeping them in school after they are enrolled. The talk of the 'hunger for education' in the villages is largely a romantic illusion, most of all in the poorest countries of the region ...[68]

These issues were largely missing in the discussion of the economics of education in poor countries, and Myrdal called for a radical change in the entire educational system. The educational reforms had to be inserted into the national development plans. Issues like 'the low quality and standards of schooling, the wastage and misdirection, and, in particular, the question of equality, which is interwoven in every quantitative and qualitative problem in South Asia', had to be dealt with,[69] and education had to be planned as an integrated whole, in terms of quality and continuity. Special attention had to be paid to the education and the social status

[67] Ibid., pp. 1776–77.

[68] Ibid., p. 1801.

[69] Ibid., p. 1812.

of the teachers and to the attitudes to schooling of the pupils and their parents, so as to prepare them to meet the requirements of development.

The Challenge of World Poverty

Asian Drama ended there. Due to the length of the work, Myrdal chose not to present any comprehensive strategy of development for the South Asian countries. That task he saved for another book, published in 1970: *The Challenge of World Poverty*, with the subtitle *A World Anti-Poverty Program in Outline*.[70] Like many other books by Myrdal, this one as well was the outgrowth of a series of lectures, this time the three 1969 Christian A. Herter Lectures at the Johns Hopkins School of Advanced International Studies, with the title 'The Rich and Poor Countries: A Strategy for Development in the 1970's'. '... I was happy to accept the invitation and to use the occasion to spell out the missing eighth part of the earlier book'.[71]

In *The Challenge of World Poverty* Myrdal drew heavily on *Asian Drama*. His intention was primarily to offer policy recommendations for South Asia, notably India and Pakistan, but he hoped that these conclusions would be relevant also for the underdeveloped world as a whole. He stressed the political nature of the book:

> This is a *political* book and should thus, according to my philosophy, be directed not only to experts, officials, and professional politicians but to interested persons among the general public. I have therefore labored to make my message as direct and simple as possible, though without giving up my intention that my policy recommendations should stand out as rational conclusions from facts and explicitly stated value premises. I have taken no political or diplomatic precautions but have tried to speak as plainly and frankly as I can.[72]

Myrdal again stated that it was not possible to limit the analysis to economic factors. The only permissible demarcation, he argued, was between relevant and less relevant factors.

[70] Myrdal (1970).

[71] Ibid., p. x.

[72] Ibid., p. xi.

> For what a state needs, and what politics is about is … a macro-plan for inducing changes simultaneously in a great number of conditions, not only the economic, and doing it in a way so as to coordinate all these changes in order to reach a maximum of development effect of efforts and sacrifices. This may, in popular terms, be a definition of what we mean by planning.[73]

The value premises used in *The Challenge of World Poverty* were the same as those used in *Asian Drama*: the modernization ideals. Myrdal argued strongly against those who held that it would be a mistake to use them, since they were alien to the Third World, because they had originated in Western countries and were hence inappropriate. According to Myrdal, this was a mistaken view. The traditional valuations were static and could not be used for determining goals for planning. '… *the idea of seeking the goals for development in these valuations amounts to abstaining from rational planning*'.[74]

When Myrdal sketched the conditions prevailing in the Third World, in the same way as in *Asian Drama,* he stressed the differences between these and those of the First World, in terms of resource base, climate and population growth, but also the interdependence between the two, through international trade and technological change. The industrialized countries conferred disadvantages on the Third World. Progress—which proceeds exponentially—was concentrated to the First World and was, on balance, detrimental to the development of the developing countries. It was largely responsible for their disadvantageous trade position and it made it extremely difficult for them to break into the markets of the First World.

In *The Challenge of World Poverty*, Myrdal strongly came back to the issue of equality as a prerequisite for development. He noted the fact that all the governments in South Asia endorsed equality, but at the same time he lamented the passivity of the masses. Poverty and inequality bred each other. Still, the masses stood out as '*mostly passive, apathetic, and inarticulate*'.[75] They were the simple object of government policy, but—since they lacked political power and failed to organize—hardly ever its subject. This was a serious matter, since Myrdal was convinced that 'the

[73] Ibid., p. 21.
[74] Ibid., p. 29.
[75] Ibid., p. 62.

radical reforms which are needed *must be carried out by the underdeveloped countries themselves*'.[76] '*To become important, the egalitarian ideals need pressure from below*. And that is exactly what is missing in most underdeveloped countries'.[77]

Myrdal singled out four different 'internal' reform issues: agriculture, population, education and the 'soft' state. The industrialization issue, which had occupied an important place in *Asian Drama*, on the other hand, was played down.

Agriculture

Myrdal based his conclusions with respect to agriculture on the low yields prevailing in the sector and the low rate of labor utilization there. This was the result of a primitive agricultural technology and he argued that technological progress must require a higher and more efficient labor input. It would, however, not be possible to take over more productive technologies from the advanced countries, but techniques had to be adjusted so as to fit the factor proportions prevailing in the Third World. This in turn called for research, and Myrdal saw research as '*one of the strategically most important requirements for foreign aid from the developed countries*'.[78] The development of agriculture also called for serious land reform, with a special view to equality, especially tenancy reform. Myrdal once more came back to the 'capitalist welfare solution' that he advocated in *Asian Drama*: encouragement of the efforts of progressive landowners and privileged tenants and at the same time employment of measures that could serve to protect the contemporary landless in the villages and provide them with small plots of land.

Myrdal was utterly skeptical to 'technocratic' solutions in agriculture. In the past, they had avoided the crucial equality issue, and they were likely to continue to do so. During the time that had passed between *Asian Drama* and *The Challenge of World Poverty*, the Green Revolution had become a big issue. The employment of high-yielding seed varieties was advocated in some optimistic circles, notably the World Health Organization, as a panacea. Myrdal pointed out that in the first place,

[76] Ibid., p. 254.

[77] Ibid., p. 76.

[78] Ibid., p. 98.

productive use of the 'miracle seeds' required a number of complementary inputs, like fertilizer, water and pesticides, increased weeding, etc. More important, however, he felt, was that it diverted the attention from the necessary institutional agrarian reforms, without which it would not be possible to progress. The mere introduction of the new seeds was likely simply to strengthen the position of the reactionary interests that dominated the villages: landowners and moneylenders, and hence increase the extent of inequality instead of reducing it.

Population

Myrdal's recommendations with respect to population policy were simple. High rates of population growth threatened the living standard. They hence had to be brought down, and the only way to do that was to work on the birth rates. '... *underdeveloped countries today can make the spread of birth control public policy*'.[79] Contraceptives could be distributed, but this was likely to run into strong resistance among the masses. Still, Myrdal saw no other way of neutralizing the negative effects of rapid population growth than a vigorous public policy to spread birth control. The developed countries could only assist with research on the new birth control technology, but the action had to be taken by the user countries.

Education

The educational sector was plagued by a severe lack of reliable statistics, but its main problem, as Myrdal saw it, was qualitative. The colonial heritage was masses mostly untouched by formal education. The European powers had created educational systems that effectively kept the vast majority of the population out and cemented the barrier between them and the upper classes. The situation had not changed much after independence. Myrdal called for adult literacy education, both as a goal in itself and as a means for making the school education of children more efficient, but this called for a fundamental change of attitude among the 'educated' classes.

Throughout the South Asian school systems, the quality of the education was low and the number of absentees, repeaters and drop-outs high.

[79] Ibid., p. 151.

Myrdal reiterated the demands that he had made in *Asian Drama*, for improved teacher quality, more vocational education and fewer 'generalists'. The rapid increase of secondary and tertiary education, which took place at the expense of primary education, must be stopped, but possibly, in the short run, given the severe lack of qualified teachers, the enrollment of children in primary education might also have to be cut down—but only temporarily, until the teacher situation improved.

The Soft State

Myrdal expanded his analysis of the soft state considerably from *Asian Drama* to *The Challenge of World Poverty*. He stated bluntly that the '... *underdeveloped countries are all, though in varying degrees, "soft states"*',[80] which could be exploited for personal gain by the economically, socially and politically powerful. This attitude, in turn, had spread to all strata of the population and had produced a general inclination to resist public controls. It constituted a formidable obstacle to development since, argued Myrdal, development was impossible without social discipline, and the latter could not be achieved without legislation, regulations and compulsion, all of which tended to be blocked by the vested interests of those on top of the economic and social pyramid. The professed desire to change this state of the arts had led to very little change. The entire political, legal and administrative system was heavily biased against the poor.

Even though it was difficult to measure, Myrdal pointed out that the degree of corruption was much higher in the South Asian countries than in the Western developed countries and he furthermore claimed that practically everything that had taken place after independence in those countries had served to create greater incentives to and greater opportunities for corruption, 'particularly large-scale graft by politicians and higher officials but spreading downward to petty bribery'.[81] The situation was similar in Latin America and Africa.

It was obvious to Myrdal that one of the most important tasks of the countries of the Third World was to combat corruption, making the state less soft. Large-scale administrative reform was called for, including the

[80] Ibid., p. 208.

[81] Ibid., p. 234.

scaling-down of the public administration, which at the time was characterized by the employment of people who lacked both competence and integrity. The situation was almost hopeless. The countries of the Third World had to fight rampant corruption when everything in their societies tended to feed it. Myrdal saw no other choice than a crusade against corruption if the development effort were not to be jeopardized. The efforts had to begin at the top, with ministers, higher officials and businessmen in collusion with these groups, for it was at the top that corruption originated. Unfortunately, such efforts must be accomplished by the countries themselves, even though the developed countries could attempt to put pressure on them to do so. Western companies should abstain from the use of bribes as part of their business practice.

The Other Side

Turning to the role of the developed countries, Myrdal emphasized that although the sweeping reforms he called for had to be undertaken by the underdeveloped countries themselves, a 'neutral' attitude to the internal problems of these countries in the developed nations was '*not one of the choices*'.[82] On the contrary, the Western countries could exert an influence by the choice of which countries to assist and of the purposes for which aid should be given. His vision was that of '*close cooperation between the Western developed countries and the progressive forces in underdeveloped countries*'.[83] He warned against direct private investment by Western business interests in countries where no reforms were undertaken, because the natural allies of such interests were the ruling oligarchies. This simply amounted to '*a direct continuation of colonial policy and, indeed, the justification for the label "neo-colonialism" often thrown at Western enterprise*'.[84]

The position of the Third World countries with respect to foreign trade and capital movements was not only precarious, but also deteriorating. Myrdal repeated his analysis from *Asian Drama* of the systematic bias of the international markets against them and their tendency to contribute to increasing internal inequality. The prospects of traditional exports were

[82] Ibid., p. 259.

[83] Ibid., p. 262.

[84] Ibid., pp. 263–64.

not bright, and it was exceedingly difficult to develop exports of manufactured goods. As a result, the gap between these countries' import needs and their export revenues was widening, and neither portfolio investments nor direct investments were of the magnitude sufficient to bridge the gap. The result was that the underdeveloped countries were becoming increasingly indebted.

Myrdal called on the developed countries to change their trade policies in such a way as to counteract the 'natural' mechanism of international trade by promoting imports from the Third World. His—utopian—vision was one of international solidarity:

> Abolishing the policies in developed countries that are adverse to the underdeveloped countries, and, still more, initiating policies that would help them positively, assume that people in the former countries would accept, to one degree or another, the conception of a *welfare world*. [...] this can be done with little or no real sacrifice in the long run.[85]

In practice, however, virtually nothing had been done. Myrdal's verdict was harsh:

> This has, however, not released much willingness among their peoples to part with what they have, or to accept even minor adjustment in their trading practices. It is a fact that, as yet, *no Western developed nation has made any real sacrifices in shouldering aid obligations to underdeveloped countries. Neither have they been prepared, on the whole, to abstain from even minor trading advantages that can be shown to be of real long-term interest to a developed country*. The trend has not gone in the direction of greater willingness to come to the assistance of the underdeveloped countries.[86]

The aid flows from the developed countries were completely unsatisfactory according to Myrdal. Official statistics were utterly unreliable. They even included military aid and business transactions, and much of the aid was tied. Myrdal contrasted American behavior, which primarily saw to the political and economic interest of the United States, and Swedish behavior: 'The idea that aid to underdeveloped countries would be in "the

[85] Ibid., p. 298.

[86] Ibid., p. 313.

best interest of Sweden" does not occur naturally to Swedes'.[87] The only reason they had was '*the moral one of solidarity with people in distress*'.[88] Aid policies had to rest on moral grounds. They could never be morally 'neutral'. In order to get away from narrowly defined, selfish, national interests, Myrdal wanted the aid to be channeled through multilateral, intergovernmental organizations.

[87] Ibid., p. 359.

[88] Ibid., p. 363.

CHAPTER 7

The Reaction to *Asian Drama* I: The West

The Immediate Reception

Asian Drama was published in March 1968. As could be expected, its publication sparked plenty of reaction: praise and criticism, but never indifference. The first round of reception was generally positive (although less so than that of *An American Dilemma*).[1] In spite of complaints about 'an admitted lack of historical depth', George E. Taylor's review in the *Virginia Quarterly Review* was titled 'A Monumental Study', and his conclusion was: 'This book represents a methodological breakthrough in our study of the Third World; it is as important for the policy-maker as for the scholar'.[2] Other reviewers agreed. John Fischer, the editor of *Harper's Magazine,* even maintained that the publication of *Asian Drama* would allow Myrdal to change the course of history for a second time, even though Myrdal was 'a painfully bad writer' with a prose that was 'graceless and infested with clichés'.[3]

Kenneth Boulding, the president of the American Economic Association, an economist with heterodox inclinations, stated in *The New Republic* that Myrdal was perhaps the top social scientist in the world

[1] Jackson (1990, p. 340).

[2] Taylor (1968, pp. 475, 477).

[3] Fischer (1968, p. 12).

M. Lundahl, *The Dynamics of Poverty*, Palgrave Studies in the History of Economic Thought,
https://doi.org/10.1007/978-3-030-73347-6_7

and praised him for stressing the role of social factors in the process of development an underdevelopment, in bright contrast to the technologically oriented analysis of the mainstream economists, and his insistence on the importance of agriculture for raising incomes. However, he lamented the lack of a discussion of tax systems, public finance, banking systems and credit markets.[4]

Another heterodox reviewer, who sympathized with Myrdal *a priori*, was Thomas Balogh at Oxford, who reviewed *Asian Drama* in the *IDS Bulletin*. He called it one of the two 'massive peaks of interpretative political economy [that] tower over the arid, flat plain inhabited by the conventional modern economists who, lured on by the mirage of mathematical determinacy, undue generalization, illicit aggregation and inadequately documented secular vistas, aspire to the status of scientists'.[5] The work was a basic source for the entire field of economic development.

George Rosen, at the time with the Asian Development Bank, writing in the *American Economic Review*, thought that the book had been 'well worth waiting for' and referred to 'the seriousness of the effort and the reputation of the author'.[6] However, he thought that it was too long and boring in sections and lamented that Myrdal offered no overall conclusions. 'The split personality of Myrdal between his broad, even radical, framework and his pragmatic, quite limited policy suggestions is striking'.[7] The latter were limited to planning, employment and agriculture. Rosen thought that Myrdal's forecast of the future of South Asia was gloomier than what was justified. He underestimated both the possibility of expanding exports and the promise offered by the Green Revolution.

Hla Myint reviewed *Asian Drama* for the *Swedish Journal of Economics*.[8] Like many other reviewers he complained—wittily—that the work was too long:

> In one sense, the title of the book is rather apt. Myrdal's rococo analyses and digressions on his themes with wide ranging references to economic

[4] Boulding (1968, p. 12).

[5] Balogh (1968). The other peak was John Kenneth Galbraith's (1967) *The New Industrial State*. Another favorable review was that by Bliven (1969, pp. 116, 122): 'a useful, fascinating and magnificent work [...] a model social inquiry'.

[6] Rosen (1968, p. 1397).

[7] Ibid., p. 1398.

[8] Myint (1968).

history, history of economic thought and political opinions are reminiscent of the erudite elaboration with which the traditional Asian dramatists treat their themes while holding back the movement of their stories for an unconscionably long time. There are obvious analogies between the length of Myrdal's book and the length of a Japanese Kabuki play or a Burmese epic drama (which used to take one whole night to perform).[9]

However, while the traditional dramas had the virtue of ending in a *grande finale*, Myrdal's did not. Instead of ending with a concluding section where the threads were pulled together it ended in 'an anti-climax in the form of a brief postscript and a forbidding array of appendices'.[10] In the end, according to Myint, 'The book as it stands will not escape the fate which Asian audiences have reserved for their traditional epic drama: to skip the boring parts and quote at length from the interesting parts'.[11]

Myint objected to what he felt was an overemphasis on India at the expense of the rest of the South Asian region and the misleading projection of the Indian conditions on the latter, notable not least in Myrdal's treatment of 'the role of export expansion in the economic development of the smaller Asian countries in a rather cavalier manner'.[12]

The anthropologist Clifford Geertz argued that *Asian Drama* was too Western centered and too moralistic to be of any use when it came to understanding the realities of South Asia. It was stereotype, abstract and unnuanced and based to an undue extent on general principles and the welfare state. Myrdal had paid no attention to the anthropological and sociological evidence of the situation in South Asia and had not spent any time in the countryside himself. His view of South Asia was 'completely stereotype'.[13] With respect to India, stated Geertz, 'It would seem impossible to write nearly a million words on a country with such a rich history, so profound a culture, and so complex a social system and fail to convey its originality and the vitality of its spirit somewhere; but Professor

[9] Ibid., p. 242.

[10] Ibid.

[11] Ibid., p. 245.

[12] Ibid., p. 243.

[13] Geertz (1969, p. 31).

Myrdal has accomplished it'.[14] For Geertz, *Asian Drama* was 'ultimately unsatisfying'.[15]

Maurice Zinkin, an ex-civil servant of Britain in India, concentrated his criticism on Myrdal's value statements. 'Once one gets away from values there is very little left to criticize in Dr. Myrdal'.[16] However, Myrdal was anchored far too much in the Enlightenment. Zinkin questioned the ethics of forcing people with traditional ideas to embrace his modernization ideals:

> What Dr. Myrdal is really objecting to is that the Indian Government is, as indeed are all the governments of South Asia, not always able to enforce on the public those modernising ideas of the governing elites of which Dr. Myrdal happens to approve. Yet such ideas could only be enforced by an almost Stalinist level of terror.[17]

Myrdal concentrated on the ends but dodged the question of the necessary means. How many little old Indian ladies would have to be shot for the caste system to disappear? Also, he failed to appreciate the true importance of religion in South Asian society:

> Present institutions ... are central to the life of South Asia and are deeply embodied in religion. Dr. Myrdal appears to have very little respect for the Hindu or Buddhist or even Muslim interpretation of the universe. As a true descendant of the Enlightenment perhaps he cannot be expected to show them much respect. Nevertheless, they govern the lives of nearly everybody in South Asia, intellectual and peasant alike. They are the cement of society, the guardians of morals, the main consolation in the distress and affliction which are so frequent in a poor society. Five-year plans are no substitute.[18]

Zinkin thought Myrdal to be 'quite casual when he is dealing with values'.[19] Myrdal was idiosyncratic: 'He would like to see the society of

[14] Ibid.

[15] Ibid., p. 27.

[16] Zinkin (1968, p. 578).

[17] Ibid., p. 576.

[18] Ibid., p. 577.

[19] Ibid., pp. 577–78.

South Asia reconstituted into something very near to modern Sweden ...'[20]

Another Asia veteran, the agricultural economist Daniel Thorner, accused Myrdal of not having left his Delhi vantage point and of swallowing uncritically the centrally professed views of the Indian Congress party in political command, while, in fact, in the countryside it was a 'self-seeking petty plutocracy' that represented the powerful in the villages.[21] Myrdal's recipe for agrarian change would never work. His call for 'welfare capitalism' would never accomplish any fundamental change in agrarian relations. The only way of breaking what Thorner saw as predatory capitalism in Indian agriculture went through the organization and fighting by the farmers themselves.

Harvard economist Gustav Papanek also passed a harsh verdict on *Asian Drama*: 'Unfortunately, Professor Myrdal has hardly advanced understanding of the interaction of social and economic factors in development'.[22] Papanek hinted that the huge work was superficial:

> It is ... no longer enough to point out that economists who assume simple, universal economic cause-and-effect relationships in development are naive. It would be an important contribution to indicate the limits of economic influence and the impact of economic factors within those limits. It is not enough to say that institutions are important. It would be helpful to know how important they are and how they can be changed, or how their influence can be neutralized if it is pernicious. Myrdal contents himself with an attack on the naivete of some economists writing in the 1950's. He fails to delimit the role of economic factors, of institutions, values, motives, political systems, or of the other non-economic influences which he stresses.[23]

Papanek objected to Myrdal's statement that Asian farmers were not responsive to prices, offering examples to the contrary and challenging Myrdal to offer precise statements of the mechanisms involved. He also took issue with Myrdal's 'cavalier neglect of numbers' and accused him of neglecting quantification 'to an absurd degree', unfortunately so,

[20] Ibid., p. 575.

[21] Thorner (1968, p. A-3).

[22] Papanek (1968, p. 308).

[23] Ibid., p. 309.

since according to Papanek, there was plenty of quantitative evidence to contradict some of Myrdal's qualitative statements.[24]

In the end, Papanek was not impressed:

> One only wishes that his book were not so uneven, so superficial, and so wrong in parts. Unfortunately, the generalist, even the general sociologist, may find it difficult to distinguish the places where Myrdal writes on the basis of a remarkable insight or about a question with no contradictory evidence, from those where he runs counter to available evidence and is almost certainly wrong.[25]

Lauchlin Currie, at the time at Simon Fraser University in Vancouver, thought that *Asian Drama* was too long and poorly organized, that the work claimed too much and that Myrdal was 'less than generous' in his appreciation of the work of other economists.[26] However:

> As against these general defects or sources of irritation must be set the undoubted merits. The book offers an excellent introduction to the particular aspects of underdevelopment that characterizes this part of the world, focuses attention on many controversial issues and in some cases advances the discussion, especially in the theoretical and critical sections of the various appendices. The book unquestionably helps greatly in dramatizing the desperate character of the problem of underdevelopment, its urgency and the ineffectiveness of the policies followed in the past twenty years. This is no mean contribution.[27]

Currie also criticized Myrdal for failing to address how the problem how the soft state should be tackled:

> … at this crucial point Myrdal becomes strangely silent. An upper class regime is rejected as is a military dictatorship … He is critical of a democratic regime's ability to be toughminded. He sees no possibility of an

[24] Ibid.

[25] Ibid., p. 310.

[26] Currie (1969, p. 167).

[27] Ibid., p. 168.

> uprising of the masses ... and is critical of a communist or socialist solution. The problem is left dangling, presumably for the political scientists and the angry young intellectuals to resolve in some manner.[28]

Still, Currie concluded,

> Although the analysis ... falls short of a new viable program, nevertheless it makes a definite advance in realistic thinking about our major problem [...] The way is now open for more meaningful synthesis of the nature of the problem and viable approaches to its solution. In this essential process Myrdal's study is an important milestone and will, it is hoped, be widely read and discussed.[29]

It should hardly surprise anybody that conservative reviewers were inclined to disagree with Myrdal's approach. A cowardly anonymous writer in the *The Times Literary Supplement* mischievously hinted that the entire exercise was futile, suggesting that the mountain had given birth to a tiny mouse:

> If greatness could be conferred on a book by the time and resources consumed in its composition, there would be no doubt about the answer. It has taken over ten years to produce, has been financed on a scale that only an American foundation can encompass (the figure of over a quarter of a million has been mentioned), and is the result of formidable effort.[30]

The anonymous reviewer posed the rhetoric question whether *Asian Drama* should be considered Myrdal's monument or his folly. He concluded that it was a bit of both. Unless something had been said by Myrdal, he insinuated, the author held that it had not been said at all, but he failed to open up new vistas. Only when Myrdal dealt with agriculture did prescriptive realism break through. The anonymous reviewer also mocked Myrdal's tendency to smash through the obstacles to progress rather than to circumvent them (whatever he meant by that)

[28] Ibid., p. 175.

[29] Ibid., p. 176. On this point, see also Krishnaswamy (1969, pp. 71, 77): '... one is left with the feeling that ... [*Asian Drama*] is unlikely to spark a major revolution in the theory of development [...] What follows from Myrdal's assessment? In spite of his many insights and acute observations, the positive thesis of his book is singularly vague'.

[30] *Times Literary Supplement* (1968, p. 1297).

and concluded that to make plans for the future of the South Asian countries was a useless exercise, since their governments lacked the capacity to carry out the changes advocated by Myrdal.

The War of the Worlds

P.T. Bauer, writing in *The Spectator*, in 1969, firmly opposed Myrdal's insistence on state intervention as a necessary condition for development, arguing that governments in South Asia were the mere representatives of factional interests, called the work a giant pamphlet, and concluded that it was concerned with the pursuit of political ends instead of the pursuit of truth—not a terribly big surprise, since in development economics he and Myrdal represented two polar positions.[31] Myrdal's insistence on land redistribution, 'partial or total confiscation', was likely to backfire, since it was 'much more likely to retard than promote agricultural progress by engendering a feeling of insecurity, discouraging investment and transferring land to less enterprising and resourceful people. The immediate beneficiaries of such measures are likely to become and remain helpless persons, dependent on the state and its agencies'.[32] Finally, Myrdal's insistence on circular, cumulative causation was mistaken:

> This suggestion is untenable. It is inconsistent with the frequent changes in the relative economic position of persons, groups and countries, including instances of decline. If circular cumulative causation operated generally, the lead of particular persons and groups would be permanent and ever-increasing and the relative position of different groups would be permanently fixed.[33]

Bauer extended his criticism considerably two years later, in a newly written essay in his *Dissent on Development*,[34] an essay that spans the full range between perspicacious observations and outright prejudice, preconceived notions and ridiculous attributions. He overinterpreted Myrdal's insistence on planning, referring to it as coercion, 'justified [by Myrdal] because of the urgent need for more rapid material progress, which may

[31] See Sowell (2011, p. 492).

[32] Bauer (1969, p. 44).

[33] Ibid.

[34] Bauer (1971a).

require compulsion unlimited both in time and intensity'.[35] Myrdal's solution of the poverty problem rested on drastic measures and he was not at all concerned with their effects on the population at large. Bauer called Myrdal's views of the traditional beliefs that acted as a brake on modernization 'unhistorical' and argued that Myrdal underestimated 'the depth, intensity and tenacity' of them and hence exaggerated the possibility of changing or modifying them through state action.[36]

Bauer did not favor Myrdal's insistence on abolition of social discrimination. The latter—'the selection of associates, including mates, on the basis of consistent criteria'—was present, not only among humans, but even among higher animals. It was necessary for 'the cohesion of society or of groups'. Bauer accused Myrdal of wishing 'to replace societies by an inarticulate standardized mass'[37]—a somewhat strange argument coming from somebody who in his criticism of Myrdal's work on international inequality held that underdeveloped economies were characterized precisely by a lack of differentiation.

Nor did Bauer have any sympathy for Myrdal's insistence on equality of opportunity *ex ante* and equality of wealth and income *ex post*. This would lead nowhere, since faculties and motivations differed, so the end result would still be inequality, and Bauer saw income differences as 'more often a condition of material progress and evidence of its occurrence rather than an obstacle to its realisation'.[38] In his view, Myrdal was simply 'generally hostile to the more prosperous and materially successful persons and groups', in particular 'the economically successful Asian minority groups'.[39] He had portrayed them as unsympathetic, in bright contrast to the rest of the population. With an argument intended to ridicule Myrdal, but which unfortunately splashes right back in his own face, Bauer turns his back on the poor:

> ... he regards the rest of the population as victims of circumstances, generally of the social environment and especially of the political and economic manipulations of the rich. The less well-off are described as oppressed and

[35] Ibid., p. 185.
[36] Ibid., p. 191.
[37] Ibid., p. 192.
[38] Ibid., p. 196.
[39] Ibid., p. 197.

> underprivileged. The latter term, now so familiar in both academic and popular literature, is a nonsense expression. Privileged people are recipients of special official favours denied to others. Underprivileged is therefore a self-contradiction akin to under-overfed.

Maybe he should have written underfed, in contrast to overfed. Bauer's views are not always crystal clear. In his worst moments, his style of writing confirms Myrdal's insight that his colleagues tended to offer their prejudices to the world dressed in the cloak of scientific objectivity.

Bauer was on far more solid ground when he dealt with Myrdal's insistence on the importance of planning, something that he had criticized already in his scrutiny of the latter's works on the international economy. His main argument is that planning, and especially comprehensive, central, planning rests on compulsion which standardizes people's behavior. The purpose of planning, as Myrdal saw it, was to raise incomes, but in Bauer's view, planning was much more likely to inhibit economic progress and development, since human beings are likely to resist standardization of conduct which is forced upon them. The compulsion implied by planning also serves to stifle individual initiatives that could serve as an instrument of material advance:

> Like most other advocates of comprehensive planning Professor Myrdal simply assumes and asserts that this policy will improve general living standards. But he does not explain why people's material condition will be improved by the overriding of their decisions, the attempted removal of their ethnic and cultural identities, or the attempted compulsory transformation of their mores and conduct.[40]

However, once Bauer moved on to oppose the argument that the planning effort must rest on the shoulders of 'westernised politicians, administrators and intellectuals' he was back on slippery ground.[41] In his view, this could pave the way for totalitarian regimes, and the role of these groups must be limited. With a wildly exaggerated formulation, certain to counteract its purpose, from his Olympic heights he states:

[40] Ibid., p. 203.

[41] Ibid., p. 205.

> The claims made by the westernized politicians and intellectuals for the right to remake man and society in south Asia are certainly not modest. Professor Myrdal writes: 'Development plans often explicitly define planning as a comprehensive attempt to reform all unsatisfactory conditions.'[42] This role is one which hitherto has been attributed to God, and even then only by religious fundamentalists. But Professor Myrdal takes the claim for it seriously.[43]

Bauer noted that Myrdal was critical of the actual planning experience in India and, rightly, that in spite of that Myrdal recommended extended use of planning. He added that Myrdal commended the planners and blamed the actors in the market economy for the plight of the region:

> Traders, moneylenders, colonial administrators and even landowners have usually improved rather than damaged the material conditions of the local population. It has been the westernized intellectuals who have been largely behind the South Asian planning policies which in India, Indonesia and Burma at any rate have inflicted much avoidable hardship on the poorest people.[44]

Myrdal's villains were Bauer's heroes, and vice versa.

Bauer did not think that land reform had any role to play in a South Asian development strategy. 'The main causes of rural poverty in south Asia are not the lack of status or shortage of land, but low levels of technique, effort and capital, and these in turn largely reflect prevailing attitudes and mores adverse to material advance', he wrote: the very same attitudes that he blamed Myrdal for wanting to change.[45] Absentee landownership and sharecropping was no problem. Criticism of it 'ignores the fact that in practice landlords often bear part of the costs of running the farm'.[46] In fact, stated Bauer, condescendingly, land reform would be outright harmful:

[42] Myrdal (1968, p. 711).

[43] Bauer (1971a, p. 206).

[44] Ibid.

[45] Ibid., p. 209.

[46] Ibid., p. 210.

> Land reform, which in the usual sense involves the partial or total confiscation of the land from those who own it, is much more likely to retard than to promote agricultural progress. It engenders a feeling of insecurity, discourages investment, and transfers land to less enterprising and resourceful people. Of course, landless workers or tenants will often propose redistribution of land, especially if it is already equipped. Who would not accept a free gift?[47]

Bauer had a better argument when he criticized Myrdal for mechanically equaling high rural interest rates with exploitation. This could be due to scarcity of capital, risk, transaction costs and lender monopolies, but there is *a priori* nothing that tells us which is the most important factor. Moneylenders tend to be villains in accounts of rural life, but in fact, they may fulfill an important function connecting the urban money markets with rural borrowers who lack the economic standing required to obtain formal bank loans themselves.

Bauer doubted that birth control, as advocated by Myrdal, necessarily had an important role to play when it came to increasing per capita incomes. It would lead to discontinuity and confusion in rural life which would be likely to affect material progress negatively. Empirical evidence was needed and even if reduced birth rates did affect per capita income they would do so only in the long run. Bauer guessed that their impact would be small, and in addition much of south Asia was sparsely populated.

Nor did Bauer accept Myrdal's description of South Asia as a stagnating region:

> These allegations of stagnation throughout the region are patently untrue, most evidently so for Malaysia but not only for that country. Their untruth is plain from most obvious evidence of material progress of south Asia over the last eighty years … In fact, the whole economic history of southeast Asia since the late nineteenth century contradicts several of Professor Myrdal's major themes and assertions.[48]

[47] Ibid.

[48] Ibid., p. 216.

Malaysia and Thailand had both progressed, 'penniless Chinese immigrants'[49] had prospered in many parts of south-east Asia and the rubber industry had been successful. Equipped with this empirical evidence, Bauer denounced Myrdal's argumentation as completely false:

> There is hardly a major argument of Professor Myrdal's which is not obviously and conclusively refuted by the experience of south-east Asia over the last eighty years or so. It is refuted also by much of the experience of the Indian subcontinent, but the evidence from south-east Asia is especially obvious and clearcut.[50]

Bauer objected to Myrdal's thesis that wealth and political power tended to go together in South Asia. In the first place, political power was not necessary for accumulation of wealth, as witnessed by the successful minority group. Nor was it true that wealth was necessary for political power. The powerful Buddhist priesthood was poor, and the wealthy minority groups were as a rule excluded from power. There was 'generally no connection between riches and political power' in south Asia, and when there was, the causality ran from power to riches. Since Myrdal disliked economically successful people, stated Bauer, he had got the causal relation wrong.

On similar grounds Bauer dismissed Myrdal's contention that colonial rule had contributed to the poverty of the south Asian region and advances his own—highly original—theory of what caused colonization:

> The causal relationship between poverty and colonial status is generally the reverse of that envisaged by Professor Myrdal. The poverty of some countries resulted in their becoming colonies; their poverty was not caused by their colonial status. Colonial rule generally promoted material advance, especially a rise in living standards.[51]

Bauer ended his criticism of Myrdal with what he called a 'blueprint for the future': an attempt at total demolition of *Asian Drama*.

[49] Ibid.

[50] Ibid., p. 217.

[51] Ibid., p. 218.

> It is … regrettable that in spite of its length and diversity the book is not a treatise on the economies of south Asia; both in substance and presentation it is primarily a political pamphlet, albeit of well over a million words.
>
> The primary thrust of the pamphlet is a plea for all-powerful government, dedicated to remaking people and society. The secondary thrust, related to the first, is the emphasis on the alleged responsibility of more prosperous persons, groups and countries for the poverty of the rest.[52]

After having noted, rightly, that due to its length, the book was likely to be read by few and re-read by even fewer, Bauer argued that the contents of *Asian Drama* were likely to be 'sufficiently congenial to important political, administrative and intellectual interests, and sufficiently in tune with the spirit of the age, to make it probable that the message will eventually be received widely, if only indirectly'.[53]

And what a terrible message! In the end, Myrdal was nothing but a totalitarian apologist for the Bolsheviks of the Soviet Union:

> That message … is for the replacement of human society by a standardized mass, subject to rulers with unlimited power. Such a society is the logical outcome of Professor Myrdal's conception of man and society. By decrying cultural, ethnic, religious and economic differences, and incessantly inveighing against discrimination, he seeks to build a society which is profoundly dehumanized. A society without distinction, differentiation and discrimination, except between subjects and ruler, would be more akin to that of the insects.[54]

Bauer insinuated that Myrdal was a hypocrite and suggested that people should have no 'choice, control or responsibility in matters which affect their position and prospects. His approach and proposals are examples of the inhumanity of many professed, or should one say professional, humanitarians. He first dehumanises people and then envisages an inhuman destiny for them'.[55] There was nothing new in this. It was simply the method already practiced in the Soviet Union.

[52] Ibid., pp. 220–21.

[53] Ibid., p. 221.

[54] Ibid.

[55] Ibid.

In the end, the remedies to poverty suggested by Myrdal would lead to the collapse of the traditional society in south Asia, with all its virtues, so cherished by Bauer:

> … the results of the policies proposed by Professor Myrdal would be … serious. Insistence on forcible destruction or erosion of deeply and intensely felt values and beliefs, strongly held attitudes, cherished traditions and distinctions, long practiced ways of living and modes of conduct, and respected institutions, as well as accepted or even desired cultural, social and economic differences, might well bring about total spiritual and moral collapse of the people subjected to such treatment.[56]

There was nothing wrong with south Asian society, the way it was when Myrdal wrote *Asian Drama*. As long as you left it alone, it would progress. (It only left a small question: How come it was so poor?)

Bauer ended his criticism of Myrdal with an appendix: 'Technical Apparatus and Some Preoccupations of the Book'. Under this seemingly innocent headline Bauer really went to town, beginning with Myrdal's insistence on explicit value judgments. This was 'irrelevant to the validity of scholarly argument and discussion', but not only that. Bauer insinuated that Myrdal was in extremely bad company: 'Nor does a statement of value premises confer scientific merit, rigour or objectivity on a discussion. Fundamentalist history and theology, Leninist economics and Nazi biology do not become valid if the implicit premises behind them are made explicit'.[57]

A catalogue of defects follows. Myrdal's value premises were hopelessly vague and even meaningless, there were major shortcomings in the terminology, Myrdal referred to situations as inherently monopolistic when they were handled by a distinct ethnic group, his vague and abstract terminology obscured and confused fundamental differences between situations, his concepts were subject to shifting and contradictory interpretations, his notion of social justice was completely vague, i.e., meaningless. 'Professor Myrdal's extensive use of loose and shifting terminology is one of the many examples in this book of the intellectual anarchy and barbarism brought about by neglect or rejection of

[56] Ibid., p. 222.

[57] Ibid., p. 223.

the distinction between positive and normative economics'.[58] Myrdal was a complete amateur. *Asian Drama* contained 'countless elementary mistakes of analysis and misstatements of facts'.[59] What more can you ask for? 'The absence of elementary analysis and the disregard of obvious empirical evidence are especially noteworthy in a book which proposes drastic remodelling of man and society'.[60]

Not only that. Bauer also suggested that Myrdal was intellectually dishonest:

> … some of the most influential and widely publicised ideas in the development literature do not represent the unanimous opinion of economists in this field, that indeed there are strong dissenting views, and that the prominence of these ideas in both academic and public discussion has been promoted by the disregard of contrary opinions.
>
> Professor Myrdal's book presents a notable example of this situation. He consistently ignores critical and contrary opinions, even when they are both authoritative and accessible. […] The critics are ignored, or dismissed in general terms as irrational or obscurantist elements, or as mouthpieces of vested interests.[61]

[58] Ibid., p. 225.

[59] Ibid.

[60] Ibid., p. 227.

[61] Ibid., p. 231.

CHAPTER 8

The Reaction to *Asian Drama* II: Radical and Asian Views

The Soviet View

As we have seen, P.T. Bauer claimed that Gunnar Myrdal was nothing but an apologist for the Soviet view of the world. With that in mind it is interesting to note the reaction to *Asian Drama* among Soviet economists. R. Ulyanovsky and V. Pavlov devoted an entire book to the discussion of it.[1] As could be expected they did not agree with Bauer. If anything, they put Myrdal in the same fold as his conservative critic. On the very first page of the book they state:

> It should, of course, be borne in mind that the limitations of Myrdal's view bind him to many bourgeois concepts and notions. Many of his arguments imply a sense of superiority. He assumes he is speaking as a representative of a more mature social system to people who have not yet rid themselves of archaic notions and traditional social institutions. For instance, when denying that Western experience can be directly applied to the situation in the Third World, Myrdal invariably emphasizes that these problems have already been solved in the West.[2]

[1] Ulyanovsky and Pavlov (1973).

[2] Ibid., p. 7.

M. Lundahl, *The Dynamics of Poverty*, Palgrave Studies in the History of Economic Thought,
https://doi.org/10.1007/978-3-030-73347-6_8

Ulyanovsky and Pavlov of course took issue with Myrdal's criticism of the Marxist brand of economics, which they thought of as completely unfounded:

> Professor Myrdal is, we would say, especially hard on his colleagues from socialist countries, who, he thinks, have a whole complex of bias to get rid of. It would be easier to argue with him about the so-called biased approach of economists of socialist countries if he offered any proof of this 'bias', but no concrete instances and evidence are offered to corroborate his evaluation.[3]

Myrdal was, in fact, completely unaware of the singular contributions to development economic made by these economists:

> To begin with, by way of demonstrating the superiority of his 'institutional' over the Marxist method, Myrdal ignores the unique studies of the life, economy, struggle and progress of the former colonial and dependent countries and peoples, which have been made by Marxists in the last 25 years. A man who knows enough of the requisite languages is certainly aware that in the last 10–15 years Marxists of the socialist countries have made noticeable headway in studying the processes under way in Third World countries, in coming to grips with their intricate problems and how to solve them. And they have never had the onesidedness that would be produced by the kind of rigid 'bias' of which Myrdal speaks in the Preface to his work.[4]

There, Myrdal had written about the quality of social science research in the communist countries with a formulation that left nothing to be desired and which once and for all made clear that he would make no reference to it:

> In the Communist countries, bias is massively and systematically incorporated in the approach to all social, economic, and political problems and has hardened into a stale dogma. In these countries, scientific as well as literary writings are programmatically expected to contribute to the fight for Communism. This limitation has virtually eliminated social science as we know it. [...]

[3] Ibid., p. 11.

[4] Ibid., pp. 11–12.

> The cramped situation of the social sciences in the Communist countries is explained, of course, by the absence of democracy. [...] It is no accident that we may seek in vain for important and original contributions by social scientists in the Communist countries to the scientific discussion of development problems in the poor countries.[5]

As representatives of the party line, Ulyanovsky and Pavlov resented Myrdal's opinion that nothing of value for the understanding of the plight of the Third World had been produced east of the Iron Curtain. Unfortunately, they state, he 'starts his work with a futile and unsuccessful attempt to "berate" the Marxists'.[6] This simply reflected a combination of ignorance and political prejudice:

> Nor can we agree that researchers from socialist countries have made no significant or original contributions to the study of the development problems of poor countries. This groundless statement shows, on the one hand, that Myrdal is uninformed about the numerous and, we shall take the liberty of asserting, highly valuable works of Soviet, Polish, Hungarian and other Marxist researchers in the last decade and, on the other, reveals his generally biased attitude in assessing the studies made in the socialist countries. Professor Myrdal repeatedly stressing his radical stance in raising problems of developing countries and defining his position as a scholar standing above partisanship in science, or above 'bias', at times displays a tendency to accept run-of-the-mill anti-communism.[7]

Myrdal's approach was deeply erroneous, biased and dogmatic. The two Soviet economists of course could provide a corrective, one which had been available for quite some time:

> Long, long before Myrdal formulated his 'institutional approach' to the study of realities in developing countries or, as he calls it, the 'alternative theory', which would make it possible to obtain a coherent and systematic notion of what is happening there, Lenin aptly formulated the principles of the scientific and partisan approach needed for making a really objective study. We take the liberty of quoting them at length so that the reader may

[5] Myrdal (1968, p. 11).

[6] Ulyanovsky and Pavlov (1973, p. 13).

[7] Ibid., p. 12.

> see how much fuller, richer, more comprehensive and forward-looking they are than Myrdal's 'institutional theory'.[8]

A largely gibberish account of 'the time-tested Marxist-Leninist theory of socioeconomic formations and structures'[9] follows, with due reference to Marx, Engels and Lenin, and a regurgitation of the party line, but without mention of any 'highly valuable' works by Marxist scholars, before the authors conclude that Myrdal's understanding of the Marxist method was oversimplified.

Ulyanovsky and Pavlov praise Myrdal when he criticizes Western approaches to the study of underdevelopment and they are of course behind his insistence on the importance of planning, even though in their view he did not understand the importance of a correct class analysis in connection with the latter. Also, they disapprove of Myrdal's analysis of the agrarian problem. The insistence on land reform—land to the tiller—was misconceived. In the Soviet Union, the overwhelming majority of the peasants had realized the importance of uniting in cooperatives. However, in the former colonial countries of the Third World, for nationalist, anti-imperialist peasant movements to become socialist, 'the numerically small socialist vanguard must support and organize them and, given the subjective and objective conditions, also lead them …'[10]

The last half of Ulyanovsky's and Pavlov's book deals with the choice between a capitalist and a non-capitalist economic strategy. They argue that Myrdal had failed to realize that this was the most important development issue, while at the same time they attempt to impute a sympathy for Marxism to him (a sympathy that Myrdal never felt). He had made the fatal mistake of not realizing that Marxism had all the answers:

> Professor Myrdal, evading this general formulation of the problem, time and again tries to start a discussion with Marxists on narrowly specific, though important questions. In general one gets the impression that Myrdal, sensing the great attractive force of Marxism-Leninism and socialist experience, tries all the time to draw a line between his approach and the Marxist-Leninist approach, not disdaining even an excessively free interpretation of the latter. This unwitting gravitation towards Marxism and

[8] Ibid.

[9] Ibid., p. 15.

[10] Ibid., p. 63.

> simultaneous shunning of it arises from failure to understand that economic development as a many-sided process, encompassing all types of production and the corresponding spheres of social life, demands the dialectical method of study, which Myrdal refuses to accept, although he cannot fail to see that it is Marxism that ultimately furnishes the only well-argumented and correct answers.[11]

Myrdal is given credit for not embracing mainstream Western economic theories, but for Ulyanovsky and Pavlov this was not enough to make him a respectable scientist. By criticizing the Marxists approach he did a favor to the reactionaries. He should have known better:

> ... by presenting a critique of the Marxists he unwittingly extended a hand to his foes from the bourgeois camp. For all his repeated statements about the 'bias' and 'dogmatism' of Marxists, Myrdal, as a conscientious scientist, ought to admit that only Marxist economists, as a result of more than a century of the development of Marxist economic theory, and over half a century of practical experience of building a socialist economy and socialist culture, possess the only doctrine of its kind for the social reconstruction of both backward pre-capitalist and contemporary capitalist society.[12]

Again, the party line prevailed.

There is no need to go into the details of the development path suggested by Ulyanovsky and Pavlov here. Anybody can guess them without difficulty: breaking the power of foreign-owned monopolies and of the domestic dominant social strata, a gradual movement from a mixed economy to state regulation, collectivization, central planning and—of course—cooperation with the Soviet Union and other socialist countries. There was nothing new under the Soviet sun.

The Western Radicals

Maurice Dobb, in a highly critical review in *Co-existence*, shared Myrdal's skepticism against established economic theory and endorsed his institutional approach but argued that Myrdal's insistence on physical planning 'must necessarily take planning in the existing socialist countries as in

[11] Ibid., p. 81.

[12] Ibid., pp. 81–82.

some degree its inspiration and model' and that his analysis in general would have benefited from 'the clearer and more fecund Marxian notion of "mode of production" and "social relations of production"'.[13]

Not surprisingly, Andre Gunder Frank thought that his own views of the process of development and underdevelopment were superior to those of Myrdal.[14] He began his review by citing Myrdal's statement that 'Even the heretics remain bound by traditional thought in formulating their heresies ...'[15] Frank agreed, especially about Myrdal himself. He was no exception. Myrdal's insistence that it was the conditions that were peculiar to the South Asian countries—their social institutions and values—that were responsible for their underdevelopment amounted to nothing but 'a cartoon-like caricature of Indian development explained in terms of the same old sacred [orthodox] cows'.[16] Myrdal was nothing but a pseudo-scientist who failed to understand that in order to lay bare the roots of underdevelopment the countries in the Third World the latter must be seen as an integral part of a system that encompassed the First World as well. The process that generates development in the latter by the same token creates underdevelopment in the former. Britain deliberately destroyed the Indian textile industry during the early nineteenth century and converted the country to a primary exporter serving the needs of the colonial metropolis. Capitalism was the culprit, and the only way of getting rid of it was the revolutionary one:

> ... for real development to occur in any of the underdeveloped countries, it is now absolutely necessary first to eliminate ... [the] capitalist structure. What Myrdal euphemistically calls 'soft states' are merely those in which the big bourgeoisie is still effectively unchallenged in doing what it pleases – playing the imperialist tune. And since neither this local bourgeoisie nor that of the United States is going to give up its power voluntarily and without resort to still further violence, liberation from capitalism and underdevelopment is only possible through popular force of arms and socialist revolution.[17]

[13] Dobb (1970, p. 66).

[14] Frank (1970).

[15] Ibid., p. 1177.

[16] Ibid., p. 1178.

[17] Ibid., p. 1184. For insights into Frank's world, see, e.g., Frank (1972).

Joan Robinson, at her most pro-Maoist, most pro-Cultural Revolution, in her review for *The Cambridge Quarterly*, systematically set China, which was omitted from Myrdal's study, against India. The Indians did everything wrong. The Chinese did everything right (as time would show, a complete misrepresentation of what went on in China). Her review was nothing but a piece of unabashed propaganda which could not have been written better by Mao himself. The scope for corruption was much less in China. The Chinese had resolutely carried out a radical land reform, creating family holdings, 'gradually consolidated into co-operatives, which permit organization of labour, investment and experiment to improve methods and a system of distribution that gives every individual a visible stake in the success of the system'.[18] In their development effort they resorted to the principle of 'walking on two legs': industrialization and development of agriculture went hand in hand. They had cut all imports except the most essential ones. Robinson could not get around the embarrassing fact that the Chinese had seen fit to spend a lot of money on developing a hydrogen bomb, but she chose to downplay its importance. The bomb was 'a paper tiger. Their main reliance for defence is on a popular army, which meanwhile earns a great part of its own keep by economic and educational work; and on preparing the whole population, if need be, to fight a people's war'.[19] The Chinese had abolished unemployment and 'the drive for late marriage and small families can reach every village and every alleyway through the network of medical services and women's organisations'.[20] The Chinese tradition was rationalist and 'it is in China that the people seriously try to put into practice the ideal: Combat egoism and reject privilege. [...] In all ... respects, like a positive, China shows the lines of Myrdal's negative in reverse. Development *is* possible, but not in a "soft state"'.[21]

Also the Nordic radicals objected to Myrdal's analysis. Swedish political scientist Lars Rudebeck took issue with the absence of international factors as causes of the underdevelopment of South Asia. He conceded that Myrdal had yielded a lasting contribution of the importance of internal mechanisms and lauded him for advancing an 'unpretentious and

[18] Robinson (1973, pp. 109–10).

[19] Ibid., p. 111.

[20] Ibid., p. 112.

[21] Ibid., p. 113.

useful' theory.[22] However, Rudebeck considered that the lack of a discussion of the impact of the relations between the industrialized countries and South Asia constituted a 'theoretical lacuna' in Myrdal's analytical schema. Myrdal did not dispute their importance, but he left them 'dangling in a theoretical vacuum'.[23] Rudebeck invoked the works of Andre Gunder Frank and Arghiri Emmanuel.[24] More important, however, he offered an extension of Myrdal's theory which also included the international dimension—the insertion of the South Asian countries in the global capitalist system with its asymmetrical relations between industrialized and developing countries. Rudebeck suggested two different ways out of the dilemma: 1) putting pressure on the international capitalist system, a method not likely to yield any substantial results, or 2) a partial retreat from the system, as the socialist countries had done. He lamented the lack of comparisons with their development in *Asian Drama*.

Jeja-Pekka Roos published a highly idiosyncratic review in the Finnish Swedish-language journal *Ekonomiska Samfundets Tidskrift*.[25] It was subtitled 'A Marxist Literature Comment'. Roos accused Myrdal of applying a 'watered-down and relatively useless' set of value premises. Only Marxist researchers had been able to make good use of explicit value premises, but Myrdal demonstrated an 'incredible ignorance of all Marxist development problematic'. Roos was indignant that Myrdal took no notice of the Marxist literature on development problems, notably that dealing with imperialism,[26] and he contended that Myrdal's opinion, that the communist countries had virtually eliminated social science, amounted 'not only to ignorance, but [was] consciously misleading'.[27] *Asian Drama* contributed nothing to the theoretical field. Institutional analysis had always been the hallmark of Marxist economics, so Myrdal failed to bring new insights there. Of course, the criticism of traditional trade theory made sense, but Myrdal stood out as a Johnny Come Lately: '… few [people] still believe in the principle of comparative costs'.[28] Roos

[22] Rudebeck (1970, p. 22).

[23] Ibid., p. 25.

[24] Frank (1967) and Emmanuel (1969).

[25] Roos (1971).

[26] Ibid., p. 52.

[27] Ibid., p. 53.

[28] Ibid., p. 55.

even accused Myrdal of being politically conservative. The reduction of income equalities that Myrdal advocated could not be achieved without a revolution. He would have done a much better job altogether, had he been a Marxist.[29]

The Reception in South Asia

In the summer of 1968, a seminar on the book was held at the UN Asian Institute for Economic Development and Planning in Bangkok. The proceedings—three comments, a general discussion and one discussion paper—were published the following year.[30] The director of the institute, P.S.N. Prasad, set the tone of the debate when he reminded the participants of the importance of the work:

> *Asian Drama* is indeed, in many ways, a landmark publication in the field of development and planning. It has descended on the scene at a time when the whole methodology of development planning is under some sort of review in the South Asian countries. Considering its arrival at the right psychological moment, one is reminded of another momentous event, the appearance of Keynes' 'General Theory of Employment, Interest and Money.'[31]

Prasad considered that the main contribution of *Asian Drama* was Myrdal's analysis of attitudes and institutions. It was 'unfortunately true'.[32] He was less impressed with the underestimation of international

[29] Gunnar Myrdal's Swedish colleague Johan Åkerman, in Lund, bestowed another review, very *sui generis*, on him in *Statsvetenskaplig Tidskrift* (Åkerman, 1970). He made the inevitable comparison with *An American Dilemma* and doubted that *Asian Drama* would have the same impact. Also, the work was far too long. His main message, however, appears to be that Myrdal wrote only parts of the work. It is difficult to avoid the conclusion that Åkerman liked what he saw as the work of Myrdal's collaborators best. He also insinuated that the fact that the research was financed by The Twentieth Century Fund had decided both the scope of the investigation and the choice of collaborators (imposed an Anglo-Saxon bias). As could be expected, Myrdal reacted strongly, pointing out that he had not only planned and designed the project but also written every single word of *Asian Drama* (Myrdal 1971).

[30] *Seminar* (1969).

[31] Pradad (1969a, p. 9).

[32] Prasad (1969b, p. 17).

trade as an engine of growth and with the failure to appreciate the importance of the newly arrived Green Revolution.

Tarlok Singh praised Myrdal for his methodological audacity:

> It goes beyond the province of any one discipline or any one field of experience. The approach must be multidisciplinary; but Myrdal is eminently fitted for the job; from the economist who wrote a brilliant treatise on 'Monetary Equilibrium' he had ripened through his successive and successful mastery of many fields, into a consummate social scientist by the time he undertook to write *Asian Drama*.[33]

Singh, however, pointed out that the production period of *Asian Drama* had been long and that 'therefore some of the data on which he bases his conclusions are not as recent as one would have liked'.[34]

The general discussion at the seminar covered growth, planning, the mechanism of development, the labor utilization issue and agricultural policy. Myrdal was criticized for basing his growth comparisons on contemporary differences between developed and less developed countries instead of a comparison with historical growth rates. The possible tradeoff between growth and efficiency on the one hand and equality on the other was brought out. He was also criticized for his failure to present a concrete alternative to mainstream development planning, for his choice of the modernization ideals as guidelines for policy—'really unexpected from someone who has attached so much importance to value premises'[35]—and for vagueness in his sketch of the interaction of the six constituent elements of the development process. When it came to labor utilization, technological progress was argued to be more important than reform of the rural institutional structure.

One of the most qualified reviewers of Myrdal's work was the Indian planning guru P.C. Mahalanobis, the man behind India's second five-year plan 1955/56–60/61. He sympathized with the 'highest sense of intellectual integrity and … intense sympathy and anguish for the poverty and stagnation' of the population of South Asia,[36] and he agreed that

[33] Singh (1969, p. 12).

[34] Ibid., p. 13.

[35] *Seminar* (1969, p. 40).

[36] Mahalanobis (1969, p. 1129).

India needed reforms and modernization to wipe out outdated social and economic structures.

Mahalanobis, however, disagreed with Myrdal's insistence on support to the most 'progressive' farmers. Such programs had been tried in India but they had simply led to increased income disparities in the villages. Mahalanobis was afraid that these farmers would try to restrict the sales of grain in order to bring the price up, in a country that was not self-sufficient in food grains. He also objected to Myrdal's downplaying of the role of manufacturing. Agriculture could not be isolated from industry. 'An agricultural surplus is indispensable for industrial progress. An increase in industrial inputs is equally indispensable for agricultural growth. It is simply not possible, in theory or in practice, to place more emphasis on agriculture than on industry. Agriculture and industry must advance together'.[37]

As could be expected, Mahalanobis also disagreed with Myrdal's criticism of the second five-year plan for not taking long-term considerations into account. On the contrary, he argued, the production of heavy machinery for fertilizer factories had been 'adopted essentially on the basis of long-term considerations'. 'It was explained that it would take at least 10 to 15 years to establish heavy machine-building complexes and provide energy, steel, and necessary capital and producer good, before it would be possible to manufacture fertilisers with the help of domestic hardware …'[38]

Some reviewers accused Myrdal of ethnocentrism. S. Shukla, a professor of education at the Jamia Millia Islamia university in New Delhi, in his scrutiny of the sections on education, blamed Myrdal for only using Western or Western-influenced elite sources, failing to provide a deep sociological probe and doing adequate field work, providing recommendations only within the existing social framework.[39]

Romesh Thapar, in *Yoyana*, the journal of the Indian Ministry of Information and Broadcasting, found no virtues in *Asian Drama* but called it outdated, failing to take the Green Revolution into account, neglecting completely the plunder during the colonial era, as well as the contemporary foreign intrusion into the South Asian countries. Myrdal was writing

[37] Ibid., p. 1122.

[38] Ibid., p. 1121.

[39] Shukla (1970).

from the European instead of the Asian, perspective of the world.[40] He did not realize that 'an explosion of knowledge' has taken place with respect to South Asia, but he was 'lost in the economic-political-social jungle' that was Asia.[41]

> The old clichés are trotted out and shot down, not for the first time. The new clichés are dressed up. The footnotes begin to tell their dreary story. This is another card-index job. And those who have read the literature of the post-colonial era find themselves re-reading the material in a kind of summarised mix. Even that old mutton, 'Asian Values', is served up and India seen as the chief chef ...[42]

Asian Drama brought nothing new to the picture of Sough Asia, according to Thapar. 'There is not an idea in Myrdal's survey of planning, labour utilization and the population explosion which has not been under debate and scrutiny'.[43] For Thapar, the inquiry into the poverty of nations still remained to be written.

Myrdal's pessimism with respect to the future of South Asia was also questioned. Rohit Dave argued that the situation, e.g., in agriculture was undergoing rapid change and that the planners in the region were a great deal more sensitive to human factors than argued by Myrdal.[44]

K.S. Krishnaswamy, at the time director of the Economic Development Institute of the World Bank, pointed out that while Myrdal was strong on criticism, his positive recipe for change left a lot to be desired.[45] It was not enough to establish that poverty and underdevelopment was the result of circular, cumulative causation. Far more difficult was to answer the question of how you set an upward cumulative process in motion. In Myrdal's view, the change of attitudes and institutions was central, but how do you explain why people hold certain beliefs? Any sociologist, argued Krishnaswamy, can tell you that this is an unanswerable question, but unless you answer it you cannot change attitudes.

[40] Thapar (1968).

[41] Ibid., p. 3.

[42] Ibid., pp. 2–3.

[43] Ibid., p. 5.

[44] Dave (1968).

[45] Krishnaswamy (1969).

In the end, as Ravi Kanbur has pointed out, 'perhaps paradoxically, *Asian Drama* appears to have been received much less warmly in India than in the West'.[46] Anyway, the fuss that it stirred in both camps testifies to its importance. Here was a book that everybody with an interest in the development problematic in general and that of South Asia in particular had to read and react to. In this sense, it was as great as any other of Myrdal's works.

Asian Drama Revisited

Given the pretensions and attention that *Asian Drama* received upon its publication it was logical that the work would in due time be revisited. Paul Streeten and Adeel Malik did so in 2002.[47] They emphasize the importance of the analysis of the soft state, in a region where no more than 1 percent paid income tax and governments did nothing to stifle economic abuses by the well-to-do: abuses hurting the poor. They also hail Myrdal's insight that corruption hampers both economic growth, equality and human development, his critique of the concepts of traditional, Western, economics, his analysis of labor underutilization, his insistence on the importance of agriculture for overall development, the truth of which was borne out by the subsequent development of the region, his emphasis on education and its importance for productivity, that of nutrition and health and the overlooked importance of climate.

Streeten had been one of the members of Myrdal's South Asian research team in the 1960s, so maybe one should not be surprised that he and his co-author concentrate on issues where Myrdal had been right and avoid those where his predictions had turned out to less accurate. Their overall verdict however—offered *en passant*—is balanced. 'Some of Myrdal's ideas, diagnoses and prognoses have proved remarkably prescient; others have failed to stand the test of history. Some were wrong, or limited or insensitive: others are still controversial'.[48]

In 2017, concentrating on India, Benjamin Siegel reexamined both *Asian Drama* itself and the criticisms directed toward it at the time when it appeared. He noted that Myrdal had been well anchored among the

[46] Kanbur (2019, p. 45).

[47] Streeten and Malik (2002).

[48] Ibid., p. 34.

Indian politicians but 'lambasted by the most learned students of Indian economics, both Indian and foreign'.[49] And, of course, he had failed to predict 'the real fissures that would roil Indian society in the last quarter of the twentieth century'.[50] Siegel, fifty years later, read *Asian Drama* 'primarily as a distillation of Myrdal's own institutional approach, rather than a prescriptive text for Indian developmental ends'.[51] Unfortunately, the work had been too long in the writing. When Myrdal had begun to take an interest in India, the spirit of Nehru and his reform ideals was strong. The perceived interest in growth might overcome class interests. By the time *Asian Drama* was out, it was, however, already overtaken by events. 'It was increasingly hard to believe this when those excluded from growth were staging insurrection in West Bengal, and those benefiting from it in Thanjavur district were massacring the landless who dared to claim a share'.[52] *Asian Drama* failed to predict what would happen during the three decades that followed its publication. Furthermore, the work was ahistorical, did not mention the existence of women and failed to specify what Myrdal's suggested big push should contain.

The most systematic retrospective evaluation of *Asian Drama* was published half a century after its publication, in 2019: *Asian Transformations: An Inquiry into the Development of Nations*, edited by Deepak Nayyar.[53] Most of the book consists of thematic studies or country studies dealing with the experience not only of the nations included in *Asian Drama*, but also of the countries of East Asia: Japan, China, South Korea, Taiwan, Singapore and Hong Kong.

The first part of *Asian Transformations*, however, consists of a more direct look at Myrdal's approach in *Asian Drama*. Ronald Findlay notes that Myrdal begins his story in the immediate aftermath of the Second World War, when Great Britain began to withdraw from Asia, and proceeds to provide 'the missing historical background to *Asian Drama*, with the advantage of fifty years of hindsight', beginning in 1000.[54]

[49] Siegel (2017, p. 196).

[50] Ibid., p. 197.

[51] Ibid., p. 198.

[52] Ibid., p. 201.

[53] Nayyar (2019a).

[54] Findlay (2019, p, 80).

Frances Stewart reviews Myrdal's methodology. Most importantly, she criticizes how he himself applied one on the cornerstones of it: the selection of explicit value judgments. Whereas Myrdal contended that only the views of the politically important groups in society mattered, Stewart argues that the views of all those likely to be affected by policy measures should be included. Myrdal relied too much on official statements, which in turn rested on the Enlightenment ideals of the Western world, instead of those prevailing among the majority in South Asia. Another, related, criticism is that Myrdal, in spite of rejecting a number of Western economic concepts, paid very little attention to the contributions of local social scientists.

The main message of the rest of the book is the contrast between Myrdal's pessimism with respect to the future of South Asia and the actual economic and social development. This is not the place to go into the details. Suffice it to say that the entire world knows that the Asian story, albeit with variations between countries, is a success story. It is properly summarized in Nayyar's own chapter:

> The significance of Asia in the world economy has witnessed phenomenal change. But that is not all. Asian economies have also undergone a major structural transformation, while development indicators – demographic, social, economic – suggest impressive progress. It is important to note that this transformative change has occurred in just fifty years, which is a relatively short time span in history.[55]

The share of Asia in world GDP increased more than threefold between 1970 and 2016, GDP per capita in Asia in relation to world GDP per capita increased from less than one-sixth to more than one-half. The share of manufacturing value added increased from 4 to 41 percent and the share of world exports rose from 8 to 36 percent. The share of the primary sector in GDP dropped from 27 to 8 percent and that of manufacturing increased from 10 to 22 percent. Between 1965 and 2016, the proportion of people living in rural areas dropped from four-fifths to one-half. Over the same period, life expectancy at birth increased from 49 to 72 years and literacy rates from 43 to 82 percent. Birth rates dropped from 40 to

[55] Nayyar (2019b, p. 7).

17 per thousand and infant mortality rates from 160 to 23 per thousand live births.[56]

None of this was foreseen by Myrdal. In retrospect, of course, he was unduly pessimistic. The Asian countries have proved capable of reducing poverty in a way that he could not dream of, from his vantage point of the mid-1960s. Thus, the poverty rate in Asia (3.20 US dollars per day, adjusted by 2011 purchasing power parity exchange rates) dropped from 73.6 percent in 1965 to 9.7 percent in 2014, and the rate of extreme poverty (1,90 US dollars) from 48.5 to 2.6 percent.[57] Reductions were, however, not equal everywhere:

> At the sub-regional level, in 1965 Southeast Asia was the poorest. By 2014, however, South Asia, which is the only sub-region that had not managed to end extreme poverty, became the poorest. Under the 3 per cent criterion. Taiwan and Hong Kong eliminated extreme poverty in the late 1960s, Singapore in the mid-1970s, followed by South Korea in the early 1980s, Malaysia in the late 1990s, and Thailand and Indonesia in the new millennium. However, Asia is still some way away from ending moderate poverty. In 2014, there ... [was] still ... a poverty rate of 9.69 per cent ... in Asia.[58]

India was slow when it came to increasing the growth rate, from 3.7 percent on average in the 1960s and 3.1 in the 1970s, successively to over 5 percent during the next two decades and to an average of around 7 percent 2001–2018,[59] fueled by the service sector, notably information technology. The high growth has, however, not translated into poverty reduction to a corresponding extent. In 1977, 87 and 60 percent, respectively, of the population was still living in poverty (3.20 US dollars per day) and extreme poverty (1.90 dollars). At present, the figures are better—60 percent and over 20 percent—but still not good, compared to the Asian average.[60]

The development of the rest of South Asia, most importantly Pakistan, Bangladesh and Sri Lanka, resembles that of India:

[56] Ibid., pp. 7–8.

[57] Wan and Wang (2019, pp. 240–41).

[58] Ibid., pp. 261–62.

[59] Basu (2019, p. 408).

[60] Ibid., p. 413.

> It ought to be recognized … that although South Asia has failed to keep pace with East and Southeast Asia, in absolute terms the region has made great strides in the last fifty years – in both economic and social spheres.[…] Slowing population growth and respectable economic growth have together ensured that … the region has experienced an improvement in living standards that did not seem probable fifty years ago. Per capita income has almost trebled, life expectancy at birth has gone up from less than fifty years (except in Sri Lanka) to nearly seventy years, and enrolment at the primary level has become nearly universal …

summarizes S.R. Osmani.[61] Poverty was reduced as well, from 40 to 60 percent in the early 1990s (except for Sri Lanka: less than 10 percent at the outset) to 13 percent in Bangladesh, 6 percent in Pakistan and 2 percent in Sri Lanka.[62]

Altogether, Myrdal's pessimism with respect to the future of South Asia proved to be unwarranted. To a varying extent, the countries that he analyzed have improved their lot over the fifty years that have passed since the publication of *Asian Drama*, using different development policy mixes, but in the main involving some combination of production for the world market and government intervention and direction, reform of institutions and balance between industrialization and development of agriculture, overcoming the obstacles identified by Myrdal in ways that he did not conceive of.[63]

[61] Osmani (2919, pp. 531–32).

[62] Ibid., p. 547.

[63] For details, see the essays in Nayyar (2919a).

CHAPTER 9

After *Asian Drama*

In *Against the Stream*, a book collecting a number of critical essays on economics from the beginning of the 1970s,[1] Gunnar Myrdal again dealt with the situation in the United States and India—the two main objects of his poverty studies. The American dilemma had not been solved. On the contrary, argued Myrdal, its presence was still felt. 'The Negro problem was … and remains today, mainly a white man's problem. The whites continually live in moral confusion. They proclaim ideals that are bluntly disobeyed in their daily life. This is the dilemma'.[2] Instead of trying to come to grips with it, the United States had first lapsed into 'the shameful McCarthy era' when 'the completely frantic idea that the few Communists in this great and powerful country could overthrow constitutional government by violent means became for a time almost a national ideology'.[3] On the international scene, it led to a policy of containment of communism which culminated in the disastrous Vietnam war, what Myrdal—chairman of the Swedish Vietnam Committee—did not hesitate to label hubris and crime.

[1] Myrdal (1974).

[2] Ibid., p. 305.

[3] Ibid., p. 269.

M. Lundahl, *The Dynamics of Poverty*, Palgrave Studies in the History of Economic Thought,
https://doi.org/10.1007/978-3-030-73347-6_9

At home, the war on poverty launched by John Kennedy and Lyndon Johnson had come to nothing: 'The living conditions for the desperately poor in the rural and urban slums – of whom only a third at most are Negroes – are for the time being nowhere substantially improving. In some respects and in some localities they are even deteriorating still further'.[4] Myrdal noted that there were many vested interests that prohibited reform, but in spite of all the anomalies that he observed, he still preferred not to let himself be depressed:

> Nevertheless, I cannot be pessimistic about America. It is not a tenable position for the United States to be that country among the rich countries that has the most and the worst slums, the highest rate of unemployed and unemployables, and the least developed health services, and that is the most niggardly toward its old people and its poor children who are so many, as well as being the country that leads the whole Western world in violence, crime, and corruption in high places.[5]

Myrdal, the perennial moral philosopher, argued that the United States had a tremendous burden of debt vis-à-vis its poor people and warned that if it were not paid it might give rise to grave social disturbances and risks for democratic government. What the country needed least of all was a violent revolution. The remedy was found in radical reforms based on the traditional American ideals, what he in *An American Dilemma* called the American Creed. The general community interests had to be opposed to unhampered individualism. Liberty did 'not imply the freedom for every crank and criminal to buy and possess a murderous weapon'.[6]

> Nor should liberty be allowed to mean that a majority of the people is left free to become ever more affluent, while a minority, and a large minority, is pressed down into an alienated underclass. Collusion between people to exclude certain ethnic or religious groups from living in their neighborhood, working in their profession or trade, sending children to their schools, or from eating in their restaurants and buying in their shops, is not a legitimate exercise of liberty but an insolent infringement on other people's rights to liberty. [...]

[4] Ibid., p. 283.

[5] Ibid., p. 285.

[6] Ibid., p. 289.

> Again, in the international arena, the United States should not interpret its national liberty as the right to do what it pleases as a simple exertion of its might.[7]

In spite of Myrdal's repeated insistence that he was not pessimistic with respect to the future of his beloved America it is difficult to escape a feeling of despair when you read his texts from the 1970s. In the case of India, his feelings were more mixed, wavering between optimism and pessimism. A mere handful of years had passed since the publication of *Asian Drama*, so the need for reform remained:

> Having studied the development problems of the region as an economist, I must stress that India, Pakistan, and Bangladesh together constitute the greatest conglomeration of very poor people in the world. India ought certainly to welcome foreign aid, provided it is given without political strings. But far more important will be her internal policies. She needs far-reaching radical reforms, and they must be directed towards greater equality.[8]

The situation was complicated by the fact that India and Pakistan had just fought the thirteen-day war that had led to the independence of Bangladesh in 1971. Pakistan and India had got new leaders in the recent past. Zulfikar Ali Bhutto had become president in the former country and Indira Gandhi prime minster in India in 1966. (Her father, Jawaharlal Nehru, had died in 1964.) Myrdal considered both intent on internal reforms. However, he expressed a certain concern that India might become tempted to indulge in rearmament and power politics, something which he saw as completely incompatible with mass poverty eradication. What was called for was mutual de-armament and friendly cooperation in the region. He recognized that to 'liquidate mass poverty and at the same time to spur economic development' was 'a herculean task', but India would not have a good future without undertaking the effort.[9] The country possessed plenty of 'intellectual capacity of the highest order', which certainly inspired hope.[10] Revolutions 'from above' were anything

[7] Ibid., pp. 289–90, 290.

[8] Ibid., p. 232.

[9] Ibid., p. 257.

[10] Ibid., p. 258.

but common and seldom successful, but the opposite—reform driven from below—was not an alternative:

> The poor, on their side, are downtrodden, hungry, illiterate, and disfavored in regard to education, health, and everything else. And to them it must be even more difficult to see and feel their rational interest in specific reform proposals. The masses are not rational on questions greater than their daily worries. Unfortunately, it is a fact that the masses are normally passive to the point of submission. Many may even consider their lowly status in society to be ordained by God, or the gods, and by their karma.[11]

The opponents to reforms had a tremendous advantage of experience, not least in terms of covert action:

> ... those in power, at all levels right down to the villages, are well trained in emasculating reforms and even turning some of them into means of increasing inequality. Corruption and collusion are only two of such means. As the reforms are framed in legislation, the laws and regulation themselves often imply the invitation to such perversion.[12]

Myrdal hinted at the existence of an 'Indian dilemma' in the context of reform policy making:

> India has become the one country in the world that has succeeded in marrying excellent declarations for greater equality agreed upon by almost everybody, including, since the fight for independence, the clamor for a 'social and economic revolution,' with policies that in practice have not prevented ever greater inequality. The mental state of most intellectually alert persons in India contains serious signs of schizophrenia, with which they apparently manage to live happily and undisturbed.[13]

Myrdal warned against the introduction of merely cosmetic reforms which would leave the privilege structure unchanged. Indira Gandhi had to face short-sighted vested interests, both within her own Congress Party and on the state and municipal levels where the reforms would have to be implemented. Those interests had to be overcome, or, suggested Myrdal,

[11] Ibid., p. 260.

[12] Ibid., p. 262.

[13] Ibid.

the development of India might be in jeopardy. Gandhi, whose aims, 'I have no doubt at all', lay 'in the direction of radical reforms', had demonstrated that she had the ability to get things done her way. Myrdal saw her 'as her country's great chance, perhaps its last, to enter an era of rapid and sustained development, while retaining parliamentary democracy'.[14] And reform was of paramount importance:

> ... political revolution in India is not a real alternative to evolution by radical reforms introduced from above but supported by pressure from below, instigated by education of the masses. The more actual alternative to an effective radical reform is to allow mass poverty to remain and even to encompass an ever larger part of the population.[15]

Gunnar Myrdal remained true to his ideals all his life, notably the call for reforms and greater equality which he had been stressing since the beginning of the 1930s and which was brought to a climax in *Asian Drama*. For his contribution to a 1978 conference in Saltsjöbaden, outside Stockholm, on the world economic order, he chose as his theme 'Need for Reforms in Underdeveloped Countries'.[16] Four years before that, he wrote:

> ... conditions in underdeveloped countries, and the suggested radial reforms, have one trait in common. They concern crucial aspects of inequality of opportunity, and the reforms are all intended to work toward creating greater equality. The underlying thesis is that bringing about greater justice by wisely planned egalitarian reforms ... would also enhance the possibilities for growth and development. Indeed, domestic reforms along these lines are a by far more important requisite for their rapid and sustained development than any favors obtained from abroad.[17]

No wonder, as Myrdal saw it. Aid statistics were systematically juggled and biased, mixing loans that had to be repaid with interest with grants and tying aid to purchases from companies in the donor country which

[14] Ibid., p. 258.

[15] Ibid., pp. 264–65.

[16] Myrdal (1981).

[17] Myrdal (1974, p. 119).

decreased is real value for the receiving country. Even worse, the official statistics hid some disastrous practices: 'Added to this is the politics of aid-giving. Between a quarter and a third of what is accounted for as foreign aid is simply part of the United States' military involvement in Indochina – going to those parts of South Vietnam it controls and a few satellite countries in the region helping in that war'.[18] Instead of pushing for reforms in line with the liberal ideals prevailing in the Western countries, these had largely chosen to support 'economic, social and political reaction of sometimes the most sinister character',[19] a fact that simply served to discredit aid at home:

> ... the discovery that aid – of the type and magnitude actually awarded – cannot be seen to have promoted democracy, peace, and development, not to speak of the false baits of gratitude and political sympathy – has tended to breed cynicism and even a biased pessimism about the development prospects of the underdeveloped countries ...[20]

THE NOBEL LECTURE

Aid was also the main theme in 'The Equality Issue in World Development'—Gunnar Myrdal's Nobel lecture in March 1975, after having been awarded the Sveriges Riksbank Prize in Economic Sciences in Memory of Alfred Nobel (together with Friedrich Hayek) the year before.[21] The lecture to a large extent focused on the unwillingness of the developed countries to provide aid to the Third World. In the United States, as Myrdal had pointed out several times before, aid-giving was motivated largely by the American national interest, interpreted mainly in political, strategic and military terms rather than by humanitarian concerns. The amount of aid was on decline and the aid statistics were the same misleading old ragbag as ever, making no difference between military spending and public grants. Myrdal considered that all this had contributed to the increasing unpopularity of aid in the United States and contrasted the situation there and some of the allied countries in Western Europe with Sweden, the Netherlands and Canada, where the

[18] Ibid., p. 127.

[19] Ibid., p. 124.

[20] Ibid., p. 130.

[21] Myrdal (1975).

humanitarian solidarity ideal prevailed. He thought that the situation in the United States could be improved if appeal were made 'to the humanitarianism and fundamental decency of the ordinary American. I cannot believe that Americans are basically less charitable than Swedes'.[22]

The importance of aid had increased in recent years, since the world economy had been undergoing a number of changes which had affected the economic situation of the Third World countries in different ways which had made the latter call for a New International Economic Order with far-reaching concessions from the First World. The formation of OPEC (Organization of the Petroleum Producing Countries) and the concomitant oil price hike had made the oil-producing countries better off, but the vast majority of underdeveloped countries were oil importers and were hence suffering a setback in their development efforts. This situation was in turn compounded by a food crisis caused by bad crops in many countries and a deliberate reduction of the food surpluses in countries like the United States, Canada and Australia. The oil price increase in addition had led to increased fertilizer prices. The deteriorating standard of living was also worsened by continued high population growth in the Third World, which in the limit threatened to provoke a Malthusian situation where death rates would increase.

Myrdal took moral issue with the high consumption of both food and other goods in the industrialized world. Economic growth in the West would have to be channeled into a different direction, one which allowed for a transfer of resources to poor countries on a much larger scale. '*The blunt truth is that without rather radical changes in the consumption patterns in the rich countries, any pious talk about a new world economic order is humbug*'.[23] He pointed out that there was a risk that the new world order would simply become 'another conventional formula' without content.[24]

In his Nobel lecture, Myrdal also came back to the need for deep-going economic and social reform inside the Third World countries, in the interest of real equality instead of mere lip service.

[22] Ibid., p. 419.

[23] Ibid., p. 424.

[24] Ibid., p. 430.

The Failure of International Cooperation

When he gave the first Félix Neubergh Lecture at Gothenburg University in 1977, Myrdal's theme was 'Increasing Interdependence between States but Failure of International Cooperation'.[25] He lamented the fact that, with few exceptions, international organizations had proved to be inefficient and could not point to any practical results of their work. At the time, the world was in the middle of the stagflation crisis, but hardly any efforts at all had been made to find a common solution.

> ... while the development in every country is closely dependent on the policies followed and the developments taking place in other countries, there has been practically no cooperation between governments on how to overcome the stagflation depression. [...] the plain truth is that each single country, big or small, has been left to steer its course independently. The pretended international cooperation has been a sham.[26]

The lack of international cooperation was visible not only in the industrialized world but also in the international equality issue: the disposal of resources between developed and underdeveloped countries. With the exception of the oil producers, the latter had been hit hard both by the oil price rise following the foundation of OPEC, by bad harvests at home, which had made increased food imports necessary, and by the crisis in the former countries which had led to a decreased demand for their export goods. Myrdal, as always, pointed to the need for domestic reforms, notably of power institutions and of the agricultural sector where the majority of the population in the Third World had to make their living. However, he also pointed to the futility of calling for a New Economic World Order. Given the unwillingness of the large industrialized countries—most importantly the United States—to provide genuine financial aid to the Third World, Myrdal concluded that 'the discussions of a new world economic order will continue to be ... relatively empty of results ...'[27]

Again, he perceived a moral dilemma, based on the same kind of double moral standards as in America:

[25] Published as Myrdal (1978b).

[26] Ibid., p. 31.

[27] Ibid., p. 45.

The governments in some Western countries, which are more committed to an egalitarian ideology, and where feelings of empathy in the poverty-stricken underdeveloped countries are particularly strong and prevalent, can express sympathy for the demand for a new economic world order and even give their support when voting in the United Nations or other intergovernmental assemblies. But as they must be aware of the consumerism and the fierce self-centered competition in their own countries between all organizational groups, including political parties, accentuated in the present stagflation depression, I often wonder how they can help [not] feeling schizophrenic. They apparently succeed in keeping their general international declarations and their national policies in separate noncommunicating baskets.[28]

Looking Back

In 1984, the World Bank issued the first volume of *Pioneers in Development*, a book dedicated to the economists who created development economics in the 1940s and 1950s. Ten of them were invited to write retrospective essays on their work. Gunnar Myrdal was one. His piece dealt with international inequality and foreign aid.[29] He called it 'an account of growing pangs of conscience'.[30] His pangs were mainly related to the aid issue:

> At the beginning of my research interest in the development problems of the underdeveloped countries, I gave unqualified support to the idea that the developed countries should give financial assistance for their development. In my own country, Sweden, I have been active urging a relatively generous and untied aid program for this purpose. Development aid gradually reached the level, sometimes declared to be a goal, of 1 percent of the national income, and it was planned to reach even higher in the future. Recent happenings in the underdeveloped countries and in the world at large, however, have caused me to doubt whether I was right. Political problems have a moral kernel, and questions of aid are essentially dependent on moral judgment.[31]

[28] Ibid., pp. 45–46.

[29] Myrdal (1984).

[30] Ibid., p. 151.

[31] Ibid.

Myrdal painted a grim picture of what had taken place in recent years. The available statistics exaggerated growth rates in the Third World. Development efforts were increasingly concentrated on industrialization in spite of the fact that the manufacturing sector could only employ a small share of the population. Agricultural productivity was low and the surplus population in the countryside migrated to cities where no regular jobs were to be found.

> The result is increasing mass poverty. Famine becomes an ever more crushing problem. There are indications that the children of the poor who survive starvation come to suffer from retarded brain development and will be a hopeless subclass of mental cripples. This increases the damage caused by the lack of primary education or by schooling that is insufficient or maldirected.
>
> As I see it, poverty in the underdeveloped countries is now almost everywhere increasing and becoming extreme.[32]

At the same time, the amount of financial aid from developed to underdeveloped countries was low, shrinking and increasingly tied. Myrdal argued in favor of a redirection of aid toward the poorest in the poorest countries, away from industrial projects, and also toward countries hit by catastrophes. He also recommended strict control of the employment of the aid funds. The governments of the underdeveloped countries should not be allowed to decide their use and should not administrate them. 'Given the undesirable qualities of the governments in most underdeveloped countries, I think this concession is wrong. I believe that the voters in aid-giving developed countries, if properly informed, would agree with me in demanding more control over how their aid is used and where the money is going'.[33] Myrdal wanted more aid to be channeled through non-governmental organizations, such as the Red Cross, since in his opinion they were less prone to be influenced by political considerations.

> To sum up, the aid-giving governments should insist upon effectively controlling the use of aid in an underdeveloped country. They should do so even if it would increase the costs of administering aid. In developed countries such guarantees would increase the willingness among ordinary

[32] Ibid., pp. 160–61.

[33] Ibid., p. 162.

people to give aid. If that type of aid-giving in the interest of the poverty-stricken ever came to be common practice, it would even be one element encouraging more democratic rule in some underdeveloped countries.

For these reasons, I now criticize myself for not having changed my views on aid to underdeveloped countries until the shocks experienced in the present world economic crisis.[34]

Finally, Myrdal dealt with the increasing demands for a New International Economic Order, coming from the governments in the Third World. The industrialized nations had, however, by and large been unresponsive. Myrdal saw the demands as a non-issue that simply served to divert the attention from the need for domestic reforms:

> Although the developed countries are not prepared to make any substantial concessions in their economic relations with underdeveloped countries, they generally show their politeness by never asking whether the underdeveloped countries do not need a new order at home.
>
> Under these conditions, by directing their interests so exclusively to this rather inconsequential issue, the underdeveloped countries have, I believe, turned demands for a new economic world order into a sort of alibi for not reforming the way in which they are governed. Any concessions they might win at these conferences are very small compared with what they should be able to win both economically and socially by the internal reforms ...[35]

Gunnar Myrdal, however, exaggerated the plight of the Third World countries before the onset of the world recession. As Hla Myint pointed out in his comment to Myrdal's recollections, between 1950 and 1975, the per capita income of the underdeveloped countries grew with 3 percent per annum on average, 'an impressive achievement in the face of a rapid population growth of over 2 percent'.[36] Myint attributed Myrdal's pessimism to the fact that the latter was in love with his own model:

> But this high [growth] is rather damaging to the older theory of the 'vicious circle,' and one cannot help feeling that Myrdal's skepticism of the official growth statistics arises from his implicit faith in the theory of

[34] Ibid., pp. 162–63. Myrdal refers to the stagflation problems of the developed world in the 1970s and the early 1980s.

[35] Ibid., pp. 164–65.

[36] Myint (1984, p. 167).

> 'circular and cumulative causation,' which has permeated his work from *American Dilemma*, to *Economic Theory and the Underdeveloped Regions*, and thence to *Asian Drama*.[37]

Myint did not share Myrdal's pessimism with respect to the effects of international trade on the Third World countries, expressed above all in *Economic Theory and Under-Developed Regions*, but instead argued in favor of an outward-looking development strategy, based on an equilibrium exchange rate and relative product and factor prices that reflected relative scarcities, combined with appropriate institutional reform—a policy like the one that had been pursued by several countries in Southeast Asia: Thailand, Malaysia and the Philippines, and above all the four 'tigers': Singapore, Hong Kong, Taiwan and South Korea. These countries had succeeded in increasing their per capita income levels which were approximately equal to those of the South Asian countries in the 1950s to levels two or three times higher than those prevailing in the latter two or three decades later.

As Paul Streeten has pointed out, 'At the end of his life [Gunnar Myrdal] turned against development aid and development cooperation, and said in an interview that the world "was really going to hell in every possible respect". But he remained cheerful, adding, "We must not let the injustices of the world take over"'.[38] After all, Gunnar Myrdal remained an optimist all his life. Being a truly international citizen, his vision of social policy and his vision of the welfare state that he so earnestly desired encompassed the entire planet. In one of his last books of essays he wrote:

> In the distant future perspective, I believe … that the human valuations that in the developed countries have brought us on the road toward the welfare state cannot halt at national boundaries. Nothing less than a welfare world corresponds to the valuations upon which our domestic social policy has been founded.
>
> I cannot be defeatist on this score.[39]

* * *

[37] Ibid., p. 168.

[38] Streeten (1992, p. 114). Streeten is presumably referring to the interview with Myrdal made by James Angresano in 1980: 'Of course, now the world is going to hell. […] Nevertheless you should not give up' (Angresano 1997, p. 160).

[39] Myrdal (1974, p. 50).

The present book has dealt with the evolution of Gunnar Myrdal's method for analyzing the causes and mechanics of poverty and with his recipe for its abolition. His methodology was developed step by step over more than forty years, beginning with his doctoral dissertation in 1927 and ending with his monumental *Asian Drama* in 1968. In a number of works, which were not all related to the poverty issue, Myrdal gradually assembled a number of building blocks that were successively applied to the subjects under study until they were finally all put together and brought to use in the monumental three-volume work on South Asia and its sequel, *The Challenge of World Poverty*.

As we found in the discussion of the reception of both *Asian Drama* and Myrdal's earlier three volumes on international inequality from 1956–1957, his approach frequently met with strong criticism, both from economists with a conservative bent and from the radical Left. The logical question at this point, more than fifty years after the publication of his last major works, then is: What are we to make of his method? How much of it has survived? How much is used today? Is what Frances Stewart stated in her contribution to the book celebrating the fiftieth anniversary of the publication of *Asian Drama* true? 'In many respects, the analysis of development has changed in a Myrdalian direction, but mostly not among "mainstream" economists'.[40]

Beginning with Myrdal's insistence on dynamic analysis as opposed to the static general equilibrium approach which dominated the scene when Myrdal wrote his dissertation, it goes virtually without saying that development economics is fundamentally about changes over time. Development is identified with growth of GDP per capita over long periods of time in combination with a gradual reduction of large income differences and the reduction of the number of people living below a 'poverty line' which indicates some standard considered to be the minimum required for a decent or dignified existence. Development economics was not identified as a separate branch of economics until after the Second World War. Myrdal anticipated much of what was to come, especially in *An American Dilemma*, where he dealt with poverty in the richest nation of the world: underdevelopment within development, as it were.

An American Dilemma was also the first book where Myrdal fully resorted to the principle of circular, cumulative causation for explaining

[40] Stewart (2019, p. 59).

poverty, in his dynamic, non-equilibrium marriage of Knut Wicksell's cumulative process with the central idea of general equilibrium theory: all the variables in the social system—not only the economic ones—interact with each other. The principle is not frequently used today, especially not in the extensive, holistic form advocated by Myrdal. This is to be regretted, for it has a place both when it comes to analyzing retrogression and lapse into poverty in such countries as Venezuela, North Korea, Somalia and Haiti, where negative factors abound and reinforce each other, and when the issue is the type of success stories exemplified by the Southeast Asian 'tiger' economies.

Beginning in 1930, Myrdal recommended the use of explicit, consciously chosen, value premises to guide investigation, value premises that were not based on the predilections of the observer, but on local values relevant to the theme of the investigation. Frances Stewart argues that the idea that values should be locally determined 'is now almost universally accepted by external development researchers and policy advisors'.[41] Yet, after claiming that 'Myrdal's method of arriving at his selected values [a method that mainly made him rely on his Western intellectual heritage] seems quite amateurish compared with the extensive consultations that are thought appropriate today',[42] she has to admit that the same type of Western, liberal, progressive bias still tends to creep into the analysis. 'And for much policy advice – especially in relation to macro-economic policy – very little genuine consultation takes place'.[43]

The problem does not end there, however. Stewart's statement omits an important fact: The employment of explicit value judgments is not the rule in development economics. Myrdal by and large failed to convince the economics profession. As we have seen, many of his colleagues contended that instead of providing a transparent foundation, laying bare the value premises would lead to a situation where any crazy idea could be justified as long as it was made explicit. They hence rejected his call. Stewart agrees:

> ... development economists, whether heterodox or orthodox, rarely analyse or declare how their own positioning, their home society, education, and so

[41] Ibid., p. 61.

[42] Ibid.

[43] Ibid., p. 63.

on is likely to have affected their analysis. Rather, most economists believe (or at least write as if) there is 'truth' out there, unrelated to their own positioning. Values are typically implicit, not laid down explicitly.[44]

Nevertheless, the principle of explicit value premises has been useful in the 'negative' sense of making economists more aware of the need for a critical examination of the points of departure especially of normative economic analysis and the extent to which recommendations rest on doubtful ideological premises. This was made clear not least in connection with the debate which began in the early 1990s on the universal applicability of the 'Washington Consensus' with its standard package of recommendations for crisis-ridden countries.

Another difficult question, related to that of value premises, is to what extent social engineering can and should be used as an instrument for poverty alleviation. This is an area where we are never likely to arrive at any agreement. It is of course impossible to argue that the state does not have any role to play when it comes to promoting economic growth and poverty reduction, but there the consensus ends, and we are back to the issue of value premises. How much should the state do? To what extent should economic development be left to the operation of the market mechanism? Which is the optimal mix? It is fairly clear that Myrdal's views were not exactly of the middle-of-the-road variety, but they served to focus on an essential component of the development process.

Finally, we have the component that has aged most gracefully of the five: the insistence on institutional analysis. At the time when Myrdal began his career as a professional economist, neoclassical analysis was more or less devoid of institutions other than the market and the *deus ex machina* black box state which occasionally interfered with the market mechanism. Myrdal (together with the public choice school) through his discussion of the soft state pioneered the analysis of the state itself and the determinants of its policies, an analysis which in later decades would be continued, e.g., by Douglass North[45] and Mancur Olson.[46] The role of institutions and governance gradually became part of mainstream development economics: What makes for good institutions that breed growth

[44] Ibid., p. 70.

[45] Example, North (1981, 1991).

[46] Example, Olson (1965, 1982).

and development and which are the factors that make states deteriorate and in the worst case degenerate into mere kleptocracies or outright failed states?[47]

Where does this put us? I would say: Read or reread Myrdal, as the case may be, but not for his predictions. Myrdal had his faults, and occasionally being wrong was one of them. But he was not alone. As is well known, the only discipline that makes meteorology stand out as an exact science is economics. We should be careful making forecasts. Instead, take Myrdal for what he was: an iconoclastic innovator who approached the world around him with his eyes widely open. Savor the wealth of his ideas. Don't take them literally but try to figure out which the bits and pieces are that still make sense and, in the concrete analysis, can be put to work. Great economists—even when they are seemingly wrong—always have some food for thought to offer. Gunnar Myrdal is no exception. Had that been the case, I would not have bothered to write this book.

[47] See, e.g., Acemoglu and Robinson (2012), for a recent example.

References

Acemoglu, Daron and Robinson, James A. (2012), *Why Nations Fail: The Origins of Power, Prosperity and Poverty*. New York: Crown Publishers

Adler-Karlsson, Gunnar (1968), *Western Economic Warfare 1947–1967: A Case Study in Foreign Economic Policy*. Stockholm: Almqvist & Wiksell

Åkerman, Brita, in cooperation with Kajsa Pehrsson (1997), *Alva Myrdal: Från storbarnkammare till fredspris*. Stockholm: Bokförlaget Cordia

Åkerman Johan (1970), 'Indiens Problem', *Statsvetenskaplig Tidskrift*, Vol. 73, No. 3, 210–224

Andersson, Stellan (1989), *Gunnar Myrdal: Barn- och ungdomsår. Några minnesbilder och dokument*. Sammanställda av Stellan Andersson. Stockholm: Arbetarrörelsens arkiv och bibliotek

Angresano, James William (1981), *Gunnar Myrdal's Development as an Institutional Economist*. PhD Thesis. Knoxville, TN: University of Tennessee

Angresano, James (1997), *The Political Economy of Gunnar Myrdal: An Institutional Basis for the Transformation Problem*. Cheltenham and Lyme, NH: Edward Elgar

Appelqvist, Örjan (2000), *Bruten brygga: Gunnar Myrdal och Sveriges ekonomiska efterkrigspolitik 1943–1947*. Stockholm: Santérus Förlag

Appelqvist, Örjan (2014), *The Political Economy of Gunnar Myrdal: Transcending Dilemmas Post-2008*. London and New York: Routledge

Balogh, Thomas (1968), 'The Scrutable East', *IDS Bulletin*, Vol. 1, No. 1, 12–15

Barber, William J. (2008), *Gunnar Myrdal: An Intellectual Biography*. Houndmills, Basingstoke and New York: Palgrave Macmillan

M. Lundahl, *The Dynamics of Poverty*, Palgrave Studies in the History of Economic Thought,
https://doi.org/10.1007/978-3-030-73347-6

Basu, Kaushik (2019), 'India', in: Deepak Nayyar (ed.), *Asian Transformations: An Inquiry Into the Development of Nations*. Oxford: Oxford University Press

Bauer, P.T. (1959), 'International Economic Development', *Economic Journal*, Vol. 69, No. 273, 105–123

Bauer. P.T. (1969), 'Million-Word Pamphlet', *The Spectator*, 10 January, 44–45

Bauer, P.T. (1971a), 'Asian Vistas', in: *Dissent on Development: Studies and Debates in Development Economics*. London: Weidenfeld and Nicolson

Bauer, P.T. (1971b), 'International Economic Development', in: *Dissent on Development: Studies and Debates in Development Economics*. London: Weidenfeld and Nicolson

Blaug, Mark (1978), *Economic Theory in Retrospect*. Third edition. Cambridge: Cambridge University Press

Bliven, Naomi (1969), 'Nowhere to Go But Up', *The New Yorker*, 15 February, 116–118, 121–122

Bok, Sissela (1987), *Alva: Ett kvinnoliv*. Stockholm: Albert Bonniers förlag

Bok, Sissela (1992), 'Introduction', in: Gilles Dostaler, Diane Ethier and Laurent Lepage (eds), *Gunnar Myrdal and His Works*. Montreal: Harvest House

Boulding, Kenneth E. (1968), 'Asia: Soft States and Hard Facts', *The New Republic*, Vol. 55, No. 4, 25–28

Carlson, Allan (1990), *The Swedish Experiment in Family Politics: The Myrdals and the Interwar Population Crisis*. New Brunswick, NJ and London: Transaction Publishers

Carlson, Benny (2013), 'Gunnar Myrdal', *Econ Journal Watch*, Vol. 10, No. 3, 507–520

Cassel, Gustav (1918), *Theoretische Sozialökonomie*. Leipzig: C.F. Winter

Cassel, Gustav (1923), *The Theory of Social Economy, Vol. 1*. London: T. Fisher Unwin

Cassel, Gustav (1935), *Liv eller död*. Stockholm: Albert Bonniers Förlag

Cassirer, Ernst (1939), *Axel Hägerström. Eine Studie zur schwedischen Philosophie der Gegenwart*. Göteborg; Göteborgs Högskolas Årsbok XLV

Cervin, Cecilia (1997), *Det illojala barnets uppror: Studier kring Jan Myrdals självbiografiska texter*. Stockholm: Hägglunds Förlag

Currie, Laughlin (1969), 'Myrdal on South Asia', *Journal of Economic Issues*, Vol. 3, No. 2, 166–176

Dave, Rohit (1968), 'Unfolding Saga of Asian Development', *Commerce*, 20 July, 146–147

Dobb, Maurice (1970), 'Asian Drama: A Review Article', *Co-existence,* Vol. 7, No. 1, 63–66

Dopfer, Kurt (1988), 'In Memoriam: Gunnar Myrdal's Contribution to Institutional Economics', *Journal of Economic Issues*, Vol. 22, No. 1, 227–231

Emmanuel, Arghiri (1969), *L'échange inégal. Présentation et remarques théoriques de Charles Bettleheim*. Paris: Éditions Maspero

Etzemüller, Thomas (2014), *Alva and Gunnar Myrdal: Social Engineering in the Modern World*. Lanham, MD: Lexington Books

Findlay, Ronald (2019), 'Asia and the World Economy in Historical Perspective', in: Deepak Nayyar (ed.), *Asian Transformations: An Inquiry Into the Development of Nations*. Oxford: Oxford University Press

Fischer, John (1968), 'Western Intellectuals vs. Myrdal's Brutal Facts', *Harper's Magazine*, June, 12, 16, 18, 23

Fölster, Kaj (1992), *De tre löven: En myrdalsk efterskrift*. Stockholm: Albert Bonniers förlag

Frank, Andre Gunder (1967), *Capitalism and Underdevelopment in Latin America. Historical Studies of Chile and Brazil*. New York and London: Monthly Review Press

Frank, Andre Gunder (1970), 'The Wealth and Poverty of Nations: Even Heretics Remain Bound by Traditional Thought', *Economic and Political Weekly*, Vol. 5, No. 29/31, 1177–1179, 1181–1184

Frank, Andre Gunder (1972). 'The Development of Underdevelopment', in: James D. Cockcroft, Andre Gunder Frank and Dale L. Johnson (eds), *Dependence and Underdevelopment. Latin America's Political Economy*. New York: Anchor Books

Galbraith, John Kenneth (1967), *The New Industrial State*. London: Hamish Hamilton

Geertz, Clifford (1969), 'Myrdal's Mythology: "Modernism and the Third World"', *Encounter*, Vol. 33, No. 1, 26–34

Gröning, Lotta (2006), *Kvinnans plats – Min bok om Alva Myrdal*. Stockholm: Albert Bonniers förlag

Gustafsson, Bo (1987–89), 'Myrdal, Karl Gunnar', in: Göran Nilzén (ed.), *Svenskt biografiskt lexikon*, Vol. 26, 144–160. Stockholm: Norstedt

Gustafsson, Bo (1998), 'Ekonomporträttet: Gunnar Myrdal (1898–1987)', *Ekonomisk Debatt*, Vol. 26, No. 8, 617–627

Hansson, Björn A. (1982), *The Stockholm School and the Development of Dynamic Method*. London: Croom Helm

Hatje, Ann-Katrin (1974), *Befolkningsfrågan och välfärden: Debatten om familjepolitik och nativitetsökning under 1930- och 1940-talen*. Stockholm: Allmänna Förlaget

Hederberg, Hans (2004), *Sanningen, inget annat än sanningen: Sex decennier ur Alva och Gunnar Myrdals liv*. Stockholm: Atlantis

Herskovits, Melville J. (1941), *The Myth of the Negro Past*. New York and London: Harper & Brothers Publishers

Hertz, Ulrich (1971), 'Två livsöden i vår tid', in: Ulrich Hertz (ed.), *Alva och Gunnar Myrdal i fredens tjänst*. Stockholm: Rabén & Sjögren

Hicks, John (1954), 'Review of Gunnar Myrdal, *The Political Element*', *Economic Journal*, Vol. 64, No. 256, 793–796

Hirdman, Yvonne (2006), *Det tänkande hjärtat: Boken om Alva Myrdal*. Stockholm: Ordfront

Hirdman, Yvonne (2011), 'Från firma till slagskepp: Alva och Gunnar Myrdals rörelser i världen', in: Annika Berg, Christina Florin and Per Wisselgren (eds), *Par i vetenskap och politik: Intellektuella äktenskap i moderniteten*. Umeå: Boréa Bokförlag

Hirschman, Albert O. (1957), 'Investment Policies and "Dualism" in Underdeveloped Countries', *American Economic Review*, Vol. 47, No. 5, 550–570

Hirschman, Albert O. (1958), *The Strategy of Economic Development*. New Haven, CT and London: Yale University Press

Jackson, Walter A. (1990), *Gunnar Myrdal and America's Conscience: Social Engineering and Racial Liberalism, 1938–1987*. Chapel Hill, NC and London: University of North Carolina Press

Källström, Staffan (1986), *Den gode nihilisten – Axel Hägerström och striden kring uppsalafilosofin*. Stockholm: Rabén & Sjögren

Kälvemark, Ann-Sofie (1980), *More Children of Better Quality? Aspects of Swedish Population Policy in the 1930's*. Uppsala: Historiska institutionen

Kanbur, Ravi (2019), 'Gunnar Myrdal and *Asian Drama* in Context', in: Deepak Nayyar (ed.), *Asian Transformations: An Inquiry Into the Development of Nations*. Oxford: Oxford University Press

Keppel, Frederick P. (1944), 'Foreword', in: Gunnar Myrdal, with the assistance of Richard Sterner and Arnold Rose, *An American Dilemma: The Negro Problem and Modern Democracy*. New York and London: Harper & Brothers Publishers

Kindleberger, Charles P. (1987), 'Gunnar Myrdal, 1898–1987', *Scandinavian Journal of Economics*, Vol. 89, No. 4, 393–403

Knox, A.D. (1960), 'Review of *Economic Theory and Under-developed Regions* by Gunnar Myrdal', *Economica, N.S.*, Vol. 27, No. 197, 280–283

Krishnaswamy, K.S. (1969), 'Some Thoughts on a Drama', *Indian Journal of Social Research*, Vol. 10, No. 1, 71–78

Kuhn, Thomas S. (1970), *The Structure of Scientific Revolutions*. Second edition. Chicago and London: University of Chicago Press

Leibenstein, Harvey (1957), *Economic Backwardness and Economic Growth*. New York: John Wiley & Sons

Lindskog, Lars G. (1981), *Alva Myrdal: 'Förnuftet måste segra'*. Stockholm: Sveriges Radios förlag

Ljungar, Erik (1999), 'Gunnar Myrdals relevans för dagens sociologi: Värdepremisser och kumulativ kausalitet', *Sociologisk forskning*, Vol. 36, No. 3, 37–67

Lundahl, Mats (1979), *Peasants and Poverty: A Study of Haiti*. London: Croom Helm

Lundberg, Erik (1956), 'Gunnar Myrdal: ekonom, sociolog', *Gaudeamus*, Vol. 33, No. 6, 6–7

Machlup, Fritz (1955), 'Review of Gunnar Myrdal, *The Political Element*', *American Economic Review*, Vol. 5, 948–952

Mahalanobis, P.C. (1969), 'The Asian Drama: An Indian View', *Economic and Political Weekly*, Vol. 4, No. 28/30, 1119–1123, 1125, 1127–1129, 1131–1132

Margolick, David (2000), *Strange Fruit: Billie Holiday, Café Society, and an Early Cry for Civil Rights*. Philadelphia, PA and London: Running Press.

Mason, Edward S. (1934), 'Review of Gunnar Myrdal, *The Political Element*, *Journal of Political Economy*, Vol. 42, No. 3, 420–421

Meier, G. M. (1958a), 'International Trade and International Inequality', *Oxford Economic Papers*, Vol. 10, No. 3, 277–289

Meier, Gerald M. (1958b), 'Myrdal on Commercial Policy of Underdeveloped Countries', *Economia Internazionale*, Vol. 11, May, 247–256

Meier, Gerald M. (1959), Review of *Rich Lands and Poor Lands* [sic]: *The Road to World Prosperity* by Gunnar Myrdal, *Journal of Political Economy*, Vol. 67, No. 6, 636–637

Meier, Gerald M. (1963), *International Trade and Development*. New York: Harper & Row

Myint, Hla (1968), Review of Myrdal, G., *Asian Drama: An Inquiry Into the Poverty of Nations*. *Swedish Journal of Economics*, Vol. 70, No. 4, 242–245

Myint, Hla (1984), 'Comment' to Gunnar Myrdal, 'International Inequality and Foreign Aid in Retrospect', in: Gerald M. Meier and Dudley Seers (eds), *Pioneers in Development*. New York: Oxford University Press

Myrdal, Alva and Myrdal, Gunnar (1934), *Kris i befolkningsfrågan*. Stockholm: Albert Bonniers förlag

Myrdal, Alva and Myrdal, Gunnar (1935), *Kris i befolkningsfrågan*. Folkupplaga (Tredje, omarbetade och utvidgade upplagan). Stockholm: Albert Bonniers förlag

Myrdal, Alva and Myrdal, Gunnar (1941), *Kontakt med Amerika*. Stockholm: Albert Bonniers förlag

Myrdal, Gunnar (1927), *Prisbildningsproblemet och föränderligheten*. Uppsala and Stockholm: Almqvist & Wiksells Förlag

Myrdal, Gunnar (1930), *Vetenskap och politik i nationalekonomien*. Stockholm: P.A. Norstedt & Söners Förlag

Myrdal, Gunnar (1931a), 'Om penningteoretisk jämvikt. En studie över den "normala räntan" i Wicksells penninglära', *Ekonomisk Tidskrift*, Vol. 33, No. 5–6, 191–302

Myrdal, Gunnar (1931b), *Sveriges väg genom penningkrisen*. Stockholm: Bokförlaget Natur och Kultur

Myrdal, Gunnar (1932a), 'Socialpolitikens dilemma I', *Spektrum*, Vol. 2, No. 3, 1–13

Myrdal, Gunnar (1932b), 'Socialpolitikens dilemma II', *Spektrum*, Vol. 2, No. 4, 13–31

Myrdal, Gunnar (1933a), *Konjunktur och offentlig hushållning. En utredning*. Stockholm: Kooperativa förbundets bokförlag

Myrdal, Gunnar (1933b), 'Der Gleichwichtsbegriff als Instrument der geldtheoretischen Analyse', in: Friedrich A. Hayek (ed.), *Beiträge zur Geldtheorie*. Wien: Julius Springer

Myrdal, Gunnar (1933c), *The Cost of Living in Sweden 1830–1930*. London: P.S. King & Son

Myrdal, Gunnar (1934), *Finanspolitikens ekonomiska verkningar*. Stockholm: Kungl. Boktryckeriet. P.A. Norstedt & Söner

Myrdal Gunnar (1935a), 'Den förändrade världsbilden inom nationalekonomin', in: Gunnar Myrdal and Herbert Tingsten, *Samhällskrisen och socialvetenskaperna*. Stockholm: Kooperativa förbundets bokförlag

Myrdal, Gunnar (1935b), 'Inledningsanförande', in: *Debatt i befolkningsfrågan*. Stockholm: Kooperativa förbundets bokförlag

Myrdal, Gunnar (1937), 'Massfattigdomen och dess avskaffande', *Frihet* Vol. 21, No. 9, 4–5

Myrdal, Gunnar (1939), *Monetary Equilibrium*. London: William Hodge & Co

Myrdal, Gunnar (1943a), 'Negerfrågan i Amerika just nu', *Vi*, No. 30, 7–8, 15

Myrdal, Gunnar (1943b), *Amerika mitt i världen*. Stockholm: Kooperativa förbundets bokförlag

Myrdal, Gunnar, with the assistance of Richard Sterner and Arnold Rose (1944a), *An American Dilemma: The Negro Problem and Modern Democracy*. New York and London: Harper & Brothers Publishers

Myrdal, Gunnar (1944b), *Varning för fredsoptimism*. Stockholm: Albert Bonniers förlag

Myrdal, Gunnar (1953), *The Political Element in the Development of Economic Theory*. London: Routledge & Kegan Paul

Myrdal, Gunnar (1956a), *An International Economy: Problems and Prospects*. New York: Harper & Brothers Publishers

Myrdal, Gunnar (1956b), *Development and Under-Development: A Note on the Mechanism of National and International Economic Inequality*. Cairo: National Bank of Egypt

Myrdal, Gunnar (1957a), *Economic Theory and Under-Developed Regions*. London: Gerald Duckworth & Co

Myrdal, Gunnar (1957b), *Rich Lands and Poor: The Road to World Prosperity*. New York: Harper & Brothers

Myrdal, Gunnar (1958), 'The Relation between Social Theory and Social Policy', in: *Value in Social Theory: A Selection of Essays on Methodology*. London: Routledge & Kegan Paul

Myrdal, Gunnar (1960), *Beyond the Welfare State*. London: Gerald Duckworth & Co.

Myrdal, Gunnar (1962a), *Population: A Problem for Democracy*. Gloucester, MA: Peter Smith

Myrdal, Gunnar (1962b), *Challenge to Affluence*. New York: Pantheon Books

Myrdal, Gunnar (1964), *Vår onda värld*. Stockholm: Utrikespolitiska institutet and Rabén & Sjögren

Myrdal, Gunnar (1968), *Asian Drama: An Inquiry Into the Poverty of Nations*. 3 Volumes. New York: The Twentieth Century Fund

Myrdal, Gunnar (1969), *Objectivity in Social Research. The 1967 Wimmer Lecture, St. Vincent College, Latrobe, Pennsylvania*. New York: Pantheon Books

Myrdal, Gunnar (1970), *The Challenge of World Poverty: A World Anti-Poverty Program in Outline*. New York: Pantheon Books

Myrdal, Gunnar (1971), 'Replikväxling Gunnar Myrdal – Johan Åkerman', *Statsvetenskaplig Tidskrift*, Vol. 74, No. 1, 87–89

Myrdal, Gunnar (1972), *Vetenskap och politik i nationalekonomin*. Ny omarbetad upplaga. Stockholm: Rabén & Sjögren

Myrdal, Gunnar (1974), *Against the Stream: Critical Essays on Economics*. London and Basingstoke: Macmillan

Myrdal, Gunnar (1975), 'The Equality Issue in World Development'. *Swedish Journal of Economics*, Vol. 77, No. 4, 413–432

Myrdal, Gunnar (1978a), 'Institutional Economics', *Journal of Economic Issues*, Vol. 12, No. 4, 771–783

Myrdal, Gunnar (1978b), *Increasing Interdependence between States but Failure of International Cooperation*. Gothenburg: Gothenburg University

Myrdal, Gunnar (1981), 'Need for Reforms in Underdeveloped Countries', in: Sven Grassman and Erik Lundberg (eds), *The World Economic Order: Past and Prospects*. London: Macmillan

Myrdal, Gunnar (1982), *Hur styrs landet? Första delen*. Stockholm: Rabén & Sjögren

Myrdal, Gunnar (1984), 'International Inequality and Foreign Aid in Retrospect', in: Gerald M. Meier and Dudley Seers (eds), *Pioneers in Development*. New York: Oxford University Press

Myrdal, Gunnar (1987), *Historien om An American Dilemma*. Stockholm: SNS Förlag

Myrdal, Jan (1968), *Confessions of a Disloyal European*. New York: Pantheon Books

Myrdal, Jan (1982), *Barndom*. Stockholm: P.A. Norstedt & Söners Förlag

Myrdal, Jan (1983), *En illojal europés bekännelser*. Stockholm: P.A. Norstedt & Söners Förlag

Myrdal, Jan (1984), *En annan värld*. Stockholm: P.A. Norstedt & Söners Förlag

Myrdal, Jan (1989), *Tolv på det trettonde. En berättelse*. Höganäs: Bokförlaget Bra Böcker

Myrdal, Jan (1993), *Inför nedräkningen: inlagt i privata registret sommaren 1992*. Stockholm: Norstedts Förlag

Myrdal, Jan (1994), *När morgondagarna sjöng. Från glömda år*. Stockholm: Norstedts Förlag

Myrdal, Jan (1998), *Maj. En kärlek*. Stockholm: Norstedts Förlag

Myrdal, Jan (2002), *Gubbsjuka*. Stockholm: Leopard Förlag

Myrdal, Jan (2019), *Ett andra anstånd*. Stockholm. Norstedts

Nayyar, Deepak (ed.) (2019a), *Asian Transformations: An Inquiry Into the Development of Nations*. Oxford: Oxford University Press

Nayyar, Deepak (2019b), 'Rethinking Asian Drama: Fifty Years Later' in: Deepak Nayyar (ed.), *Asian Transformations: An Inquiry Into the Development of Nations*. Oxford: Oxford University Press

Nilsson, Jan Olof (1994), *Alva Myrdal – en virvel i den moderna strömmen*. Stockholm och Stegah: Brutus Östlings Bokförlag Symposion

Nordin, Svante (1983), *Från Hägerström till Hedenius: Den moderna svenska filosofin*. Bodafors: Doxa

North, Douglass C. (1981), *Structure and Change in Economic History*. New York and London: W.W. Norton & Company

North, Douglass C. (1991), *Institutions, Institutional Change and Economic Performance*. Cambridge: Cambridge University Press

Olson, Mancur (1965), *The Logic of Collective Action. Public Goods and the Theory of Groups*. New Haven, CT and London: Yale University Press

Olson, Mancur (1982), *The Rise and Decline of Nations: Economic Growth, Stagflation, and Social Rigidities*. New Haven, CT and London: Yale University Press

Osmani, S.R. (2019), 'South Asia', in: Deepak Nayyar (ed.), *Asian Transformations: An Inquiry Into the Development of Nations*. Oxford: Oxford University Press

Palander, Tord (1941), 'Om "Stockholmsskolans" begrepp och metoder: Metodologiska reflexioner kring Myrdals "Monetary Equilibrium"', *Ekonomisk Tidskrift*, Vol. 43, No. 1, 86–143

Papanek, Gustav F. (1968), 'Asian Drama: An Inquiry into the Poverty of Nations, Vols I, II, and III', *American Journal of Sociology*, Vol. 74, No. 3, 308–310

Peltier, Jacques (1992), 'Myrdal and Value Loaded Concepts', in: Gilles Dostaler, Diane Ethier and Laurent Lepage (eds), *Gunnar Myrdal and His Works*. Montreal: Harvest House

Popenoe, David (1988), *Disturbing the Nest: Family Change and Decline in Modern Society*. New York: Aldine de Gruyter

Prasad, P.S.N. (1969a), 'Introductory Comments', in: *Seminar on Gunnar Myrdal's Asian Drama*, UN Asian Institute for Economic Development and Planning, *Occasional Papers*, Vol. 1, No. 1. Bangkok: UN Asian Institute for Economic Development and Planning

Prasad, P.S.N. (1969b), 'An Overall Appraisal', in: *Seminar on Gunnar Myrdal's Asian Drama*, UN Asian Institute for Economic Development and Planning, *Occasional Papers*, Vol. 1, No. 1. Bangkok: UN Asian Institute for Economic Development and Planning

Rivarola, Andrés and Appelqvist, Örjan (2011), 'Prebisch and Myrdal: Development Economics in the Core and on the Periphery', *Journal of Global History*, Vol. 6, No. 1, 29–52

Robinson, Joan (1973), 'The Poverty of Nations', *Collected Economic Papers*, Vol. IV. Oxford, Basil Blackwell. Originally published in *The Cambridge Quarterly*, Vol. 3, No. 4, 1968, 381–389

Roos, Jeja-Pekka (1971), 'Asiatiskt drama', *Ekonomiska Samfundets Tidskrift*, Third Series, Vol. 24, No 1, 51–58

Rosen, George (1968), Review of *Asian Drama*, *American Economic Review*, Vol. 58, No. 5, 1397–1401

Rosier, Michel (1992), 'On the Hypothetical Character of "Moral Premises"', in: Gilles Dostaler, Diane Ethier and Laurent Lepage (eds), *Gunnar Myrdal and His Works*. Montreal: Harvest House

Rudebeck, Lars (1970), 'Myrdals Asian Drama. Om underutvecklingens orsaker', *Häften för kritiska studier*, Vol. 3, No. 1, 19–30, 47

Seccareccia, Mario (1992), 'Wicksellianism, Myrdal and the Monetary Explanation of Cyclical Crises', in: Gilles Dostaler, Diane Ethier and Laurent Lepage (eds), *Gunnar Myrdal and His Works*. Montreal: Harvest House

Seminar on Gunnar Myrdal's Asian Drama (1969), UN Asian Institute for Economic Development and Planning, *Occasional Papers*, Vol. 1, No. 1. Bangkok: UN Asian Institute for Economic Development and Planning

Shukla, S. (1970), 'Planning and Educational Development', *Indian Educational Review*, Vol. 5, Nr. 2, 156–165

Siegel, Benjamin (2017), 'Asian Drama Revisited', *Humanity*, Vol. 8, No. 1, 195–205

Singh, Tarlokh (1969), 'An Overall Appraisal', in: *Seminar on Gunnar Myrdal's Asian Drama*, UN Asian Institute for Economic Development and Planning, *Occasional Papers*, Vol. 1, No. 1. Bangkok: UN Asian Institute for Economic Development and Planning

SOU [Statens offentliga utredningar] 1933:14, *Undersökning rörande behovet av en utvidgning av bostadsstatistiken jämte vissa därmed förbundna bostadspolitiska frågor*. Stockholm: Isaac Marcus Boktryckeri-aktiebolag

SOU [Statens offentliga utredningar] 1936:50, *Betänkande i sexualfrågan avgivet av Befolkningskommissionen*. Stockholm: Isaac Marcus Boktryckeri-aktiebolag

Southern, David W. (1987), *Gunnar Myrdal and Black-White Relations: The Use and Abuse of* An American Dilemma, *1944–69*. Baton Rouge, LA and London: Louisiana State University Press

Sowell, Thomas (2011), *Intellectuals and Society*. Revised and Enlarged Edition. New York: Basic Books

Sterner, Richard (1971), 'Klassiskt amerikanskt dilemma', in: Ulrich Hertz (ed.), *Alva och Gunnar Myrdal i fredens tjänst*. Stockholm: Rabén & Sjögren

Stewart, Francis (2019), 'Myrdal's Methodology and Approach Revisited', in: Deepak Nayyar (ed.), *Asian Transformations: An Inquiry Into the Development of Nations*. Oxford: Oxford University Press

Streeten, Paul (1992), 'Myrdal, the Man and the Theorist', in: Gilles Dostaler, Diane Ethier and Laurent Lepage (eds), *Gunnar Myrdal and His Works*. Montreal: Harvest House

Streeten, Paul and Malik, Adeel (2002), 'Asian Drama Revisited', in: Khadidja Haq (ed.), *The South Asian Challenge*. Oxford: Oxford University Press

Svennilson, Ingvar (1954), *Growth and Stagnation in the European Economy*. Genève: United Nations Commission for Europe

Swan, Trevor W. (1962), 'Circular Causation', *Economic Record*, Vol. 38, No. 83, 421–426

Swedberg, Richard (1990), 'Introduction to the Transaction Edition', in: Gunnar Myrdal, *The Political Element in the Development of Economic Theory*. New Brunswick, NJ: Transaction Publishers

Taylor, George E. (1968) 'A Monumental Study', *Virginia Quarterly Review*, Vol. 44, No. 3, 474–477

Thapar, Romesh (1968), 'Poverty of Nations or Notions', *Yoyana*, 12 May, 2–6, 31

Thorner, Daniel (1968), 'Predatory Capitalism in Indian Agriculture', *Economic and Political Weekly*, Vol. 3, No. 43, A3–A4

The Times Literary Supplement (1968), 'Modernize or Perish', 21 November, 1297–1299

Toner, Phillip (1999), *Main Currents in Cumulative Causation: The Dynamics of Growth and Development*. Houndmills, Basingstoke: Macmillan Press

Ulyanovsky, R. and Pavlov, V. (1973), *Asian Dilemma: A Soviet View and Myrdal's Concept*. Moscow: Progress Publishers

Van Loo, Ina Kay (1989), *Gunnar Myrdal's Unique Approach to Problems of Economic Development*. New York: Vantage Press

Velupillai, Kumaraswamy (1992), 'Reflections on Gunnar Myrdal's Contributions to Economic Theory', in: Gilles Dostaler, Diane Ethier and Laurent Lepage (eds), *Gunnar Myrdal and His Works*. Montreal: Harvest House

Vinterhed, Kerstin (2003), *Kärlek i tjugonde seklet: En biografi över Alva och Gunnar Myrdal*. Stockholm: Atlas

von Mises, Ludwig (1954), 'Myrdal's Economics', *The Freeman*, Vol. 4, No. 14, 496

Wallner, Margit (1961), *Axel Hägerström. Människan som få kände*. Stockholm: Natur & Kultur

Wan, Guaghua and Wang, Chen (2019), 'Poverty and Inequality', in: Deepak Nayyar (ed.), *Asian Transformations: An Inquiry Into the Development of Nations*. Oxford: Oxford University Press

Wicksell, Knut (1898), *Geldzins und Güterpreise. Eine Studie über den Tauschwert des Geldes bestimmenden Ursachen*. Jena: Verlag von Gustav Fischer

Wicksell, Knut (1906), *Föreläsningar i nationalekonomi II: Om penningar och kredit*. Stockholm: Fritzes

Wicksell, Knut (1935), *Lectures on Political Economy. Volume II: Money*. London: George Routledge and Sons

Wicksell, Knut (1936), *Interest and Prices: A Study of the Causes Regulating the Value of Money*. London: Macmillan and Co

Wigforss, Ernst (1980), *Ernst Wigforss skrifter i urval IX. Minnen 3*. Stockholm: Tidens Förlag

Zinkin, Maurice (1968), 'South Asia's Economic Transformation: The Myrdal Thesis', *Pacific Affairs*, Vol. 41, No. 4, 575–579

Index

M. Lundahl, *The Dynamics of Poverty*, Palgrave Studies in the History of Economic Thought,
https://doi.org/10.1007/978-3-030-73347-6

The manufacturer's authorised representative in the EU is Springer Nature Customer Service Centre GmbH, Europaplatz 3, 69115 Heidelberg, Germany. If you have any concerns regarding our products, please contact ProductSafety@springernature.com

Printed and bound by CPI Group (UK) Ltd, Croydon, CR0 4YY
30/09/2026
02225698-0005